The Heart of a Hero

*My Journey from Vietnam to
the World Trade Center Bombing
to the 9/11 Tragedy*

LT. Cl — P—g Let —
F O N y

Clarence Singleton

ISBN: 9781928662877
Palari Publishing
Richmond, VA
www.palaribooks.com

www.TheHeartofaHero.com
Produced in the United States of America.

Table of Contents

Dedication

To my mother who taught me by her example to work hard,
be kind, helpful, and respect others.

To my children for understanding
and for providing support during difficult times.

To my grandchildren and grandchildren to come.

To all of America's heroes who suffer in silence,
and to the memory of America's fallen heroes
and first responders who perished on September 11, 2001.

Acknowledgments

To family and friends for planting the seed
that inspired me to write this book.
Thank you for your loving support
and encouragement along the way.
It has been a wonderful journey.

Preface

Don't quit before the miracle happens.
~*Author Unknown*

Clarence in Marine Corps training at Parris Island, SC.

As I write my memoir, there are events I survived that carry with them graphic images in my mind of fire, bombs, crashing buildings, racism, and the day-to-day struggle with post-traumatic stress disorder (PTSD). I can't tell my story without sharing the events of 9/11 that I experienced as a first responder because I carry the horrors of that day in my heart and in my mind. It doesn't go away. Neither do my experiences as a U.S. Marine in Vietnam or my memories of a very hard-scrabble childhood in the deep recesses of rural South Carolina.

Sometimes it can seem like darkness is stronger than light. Certainly, as a nation, we questioned that after 9/11. But as a nation, we survived. In those days following the terrible tragedy, New York City was a changed place. Yes, we were in the grips of grief, but we were also gentler. In a city where, often, people mistrust each other, a busy city that—particularly to visitors who have never experienced the "city that never sleeps"—seems cold and impersonal, people were more patient, were kinder, stopped in the midst of tragedy to help each other.

I think that light is stronger than darkness. I like to think that hope is stronger than fear. That hope and love and faith are a trinity stronger than war. That they are stronger than the forces of racial hatred and prejudice. Stronger than personal demons. That they are stronger than any one man—or any terrorist organization.

As I pondered the writing of my story, I thought of a mantra, sort of a personal slogan that I carry with me as I go through my life. A theme of sorts. What comes to mind is what I tell myself when times are difficult.

Don't quit before the miracle happens.

I have heard that particular phrase in support groups, and it's something I suppose I've always believed. I was raised by a woman of faith, and sometimes faith, in the poverty of my childhood, was all we had.

If the Lord takes you to it, He'll take you through it.

I believe that too. God hasn't taken me this far in life to let me go now.

So I carry these messages with me, in my heart. And I hope that even in the midst of reading about the traumas against our nation, you will remember that there is hope even in the darkest times—of our nation, and in each of our lives.

I survived 9/11 for a reason. I believe that. And even though crowds or loud noises, the wail of a siren, or other sights, smells, and sounds can evoke in me a terrible reaction, I try to always remember to pray and to have hope.

I have always been a man who answered the call of duty. That commitment to help others has taken a toll on me physically, psychologically, and emotionally. By the same token, I know I have a purpose. I didn't always know it. But I do now.

The fact that I survived everything I have lived through is a miracle in and of itself. But in all our lives there are moments of darkness—the valley of the shadow of death. And inside each of us, we must hold on. Until the miracle.

I hope as you read, you will go on this journey with me. Together, let's await the miracle.

Chapter One -
The Day that Changed the World

God places the heaviest burdens on
those who can carry its weight.
~**Reggie White**

The view from the World Trade Center observation deck.

I was there.
Ground Zero.
Even today, I almost whisper those words, not unlike a prayer.

As a nation and the entire world watched the Twin Towers collapse on September 11, 2001, I stood amidst the debris, every nerve on fire, shock and horror on my face. All of us, everyone from schoolchildren to the very old who were alive on that day, know where we were when the first plane struck.

Every television was tuned to the coverage 24/7. Every car radio. Urgent prayers were being offered up in churches and synagogues and houses of worship across the United States and around the world. As a nation, it slowly and yet in a very visceral way emerged that we were under attack on our own shores. Though I had fought as a Marine in Vietnam, had been a twenty-two-year veteran of the New York City Fire Department, nothing could have prepared me for that day.

The difference for me was that as the solemn and anxious people in the Towers made their way down the crowded stairwells, desperate to get out alive, some of them even gruesomely leaping from windows, I was desperate to *climb* those same stairwells. I was there, at Ground Zero, hoping for a miracle, willing to do my duty to create whatever miracles there were to pull from that rubble. I was there to help my brothers and sisters in the New York City Fire Department, the very department I had retired from a year before after over twenty years on the job.

The day had started ordinarily enough. Like those people in the Towers, who had kissed their loved ones good-bye, who had boarded subway cars and buses and climbed into cars for their morning commute, who had walked down the gangway to planes, reclined in their seats and assumed all was right with the world, I too had started my day in the most typical way.

At 8:00 that morning, I had arrived at my dear friend MaryAnn's place and called her on my cell phone to let her know that I was waiting outside. Moments later she came out of her house and got into the car, and I had driven her to the school where she worked. Though I had retired from the fire department, I wanted to stay active and so I worked part-time as a mortgage inspector. I was as familiar with the city of Manhattan as I was the back of my hand, so the job—visiting construction sites throughout New York—was a perfect fit for me.

About two miles from MaryAnn's school, I happened to glance to my left. From that location in Brooklyn, I could look over into Manhattan, could take in the beauty of her skyline—which course now is forever altered. I was surprised to see a black plume of smoke emanating from a building somewhere in Manhattan. "Something's cooking over there," I said, which in firefighter terms means something is burning. Even though I was a retired firefighter, I am and always have been a "rescuer" at heart, and the smoke immediately caught my attention. Even though I wasn't answering a firehouse call, my body and brain immediately went "on alert."

After dropping off MaryAnn, I tuned my car radio to a news station out of curiosity as I continued on toward my planned stop. I don't know how much time passed, but I remember hearing the newscaster report that a plane had hit one of the World Trade Center Towers. At the time I didn't give it much thought, but realized that this incident must somehow be connected to the black plume of smoke I had seen over Manhattan just moments earlier. The reporter offered no other information so I assumed it was just a small plane that strayed off course and hit one of the Towers by accident.

Soon, it became clear something far more serious, something unimaginable was behind that black plume. I tried to comprehend what was being said. Planes. Planes *intentionally* flown into the Towers—first the North Tower, and then about twenty minutes later the South Tower. One Tower was shocking enough, but this coordinated attack obviously meant something so sinister that it was impossible to take it in. In fact, I think so much of our world and our thinking was defined that day. *Before* 9/11 we could not comprehend such a heinous act. *After* 9/11, we know this kind of evil is possible in our world.

My brain struggled with this reality. The questions that raced through my mind were very much like those of everyone that day. First a *what? What happened?* Then it soon turned to a *how? How had someone—in fact more than one person—hijacked a massive plane? Flown it into a landmark?* And then, of course, *why? Why would someone—or a group of people—do something so utterly heinous?*

But then, for me, the questions, in essence stopped—it was time to take action. I soon, based on the news, had some inkling of the seriousness of the situation that was unfolding in Manhattan. Retired or not ... duty called. It was and is an instinctive part of me. In the Marines, we were trained to never leave one of our own on the battlefield. Facing down the enemy, summoning courage from wherever it is courage resides—heart or soul or both—was part of my upbringing, my service to my country, and my service to my city as I fought fires.

I immediately headed back to my Brooklyn apartment, hurriedly changing clothes and mentally preparing to make my way to the tip of New York City to the Towers. At that point, they were still standing, but they were in flames, billowing plumes of black smoke spewing across the sky.

I dressed quickly, methodically running through a checklist in my head of what I might need. Just then, my son Cody who lived in North Carolina called me and asked what was going on up there in New York. My son knew that I was always helping people, and he knew I was a rescuer at heart. While I was in the process of explaining as much as I knew about the situation to him, he wanted me to stay right where I was—in my apartment. Safe.

"Daddy, you're retired already. Don't go over there." I heard the worry in his voice. It was a plea, really.

But I told him, "Cody, I *have to* go." Firefighting was still such a part of me, and it was in my blood. Duty was calling, and I just had to go over and help out.

I ended my conversation with Cody quickly. Then I ran down to the garage and jumped into my car. I headed over to the subway, knowing that when there is something going on in Manhattan, there would be a lot of traffic on the streets. My fastest option was probably below the surface of the city, not above it. I knew I probably wouldn't be able to get near the scene if I attempted to drive there. With caution, I ran the red light on the corner near my apartment building. I had to get to the site of the World Trade Center as quickly as possible.

I learned that my oldest son, Clarence Jevon, was also trying to contact me throughout the morning, but he was not able to do so because of the volume of calls that people were making. In addition some cell phone equipment was located on top of the World Trade Center and was destroyed in the collapse. Members of my own family—and the families of thousands upon thousands of others—were frantic. Of course, so many people never got the chance to speak to their loved ones again.

Moments later I parked my car near the entrance to the subway on one of the local streets and boarded the train. In Brooklyn the subway is located underground. When you get to the Manhattan Bridge, the train comes out of the tunnel and continues on an elevated track across the bridge. Besides the subway train, the bridge is also used for cars and trucks crossing at the same time. As the train came out of the tunnel and started over the bridge, I was standing in the subway car gazing at the smoke-filled sky above the World Trade Center. The majority of passengers on the train were also looking in the same direction with a sense of cautious curiosity on their faces. I was wearing my fire department T-shirt so some of the passengers asked me if the burning Tower was going to fall. I responded with confidence, "No ... No way." I had fought many fires in high-rise buildings during my twenty-two-year career as a firefighter. In each instance, we would just go up to the floor the fire was on, extinguish the blaze, and go back to the firehouse. I assumed it was going to be as simple as that.

I couldn't have been more wrong.

Chapter Two - The Collapse

Tonight, I ask for your prayers for all those who grieve, for the children whose worlds have been shattered, for all whose sense of safety and security has been threatened.
~President George W. Bush, September 11, 2001

The devastation in New York City on 9/11/01.

No firefighter goes out on a call with the intention of being killed.

But we know that every call we respond to has that potential. We might not come home again.

My faith has been an integral part of my life. The one verse that has often stood out to me in relation to my work as a firefighter is 1 John 3:16, which reads, "This is how we know what love is. Jesus Christ laid down His life for us, and we ought to lay down our lives for our brothers." I've lost friends to emergency calls, and I've seen the reality of the death, but the call to help the helpless was louder than the threat of danger. I've always been willing to lay down my own life to help others—whether in the wet jungles of Vietnam or the fiery blazes of New York City. September 11th was no different—and yet of course, in every way it was different. The world had never seen such an act of terrorism.

As the train wound its way toward Manhattan, I didn't realize it at the time, but nothing I have ever experienced could have prepared me for what I was about to see. The expanding clouds of smoke above the Twin Towers of the World Trade Center didn't reveal what kind of fire was blazing below: a fire so hot that it would melt steel and bring down two of the most recognizable icons of the New York City skyline.

As I was looking out of the window of the subway car, I could see both buildings still standing, but they were burning. In addition, the train kept on going when we approached the station nearest to the World Trade Center because it was too close to the site, and a tragedy of immeasurable dimension was unfolding above on the streets of Manhattan. The subway kept rolling until it reached the next-nearest station—Canal Street—where they dropped us off. Faces were somber. People were starting to grasp that an unimaginable event had occurred.

When the train pulled into the station with a whoosh, I got off and started walking toward the World Trade Center site. Around me, I saw people speaking urgently into cell phones—those that could get through—trying to assure loved ones they were safe in the midst of chaos. Others were pressing buttons on their phones trying—with no success—to get word out to family and friends.

I moved along at a fast pace, but it took several minutes to reach the site of the tragedy. The area was heavily congested with people who were trying to leave as fast as possible. Almost everyone was headed in the opposite direction—away from the site. Ash and soot were starting to rain down from the sky, and the air had the acrid smell of fuel burning and fire. Faces were grim, as if we understood our nation was now involved in a war of sorts.

Several blocks away from the actual buildings, I spotted faces that I recognized. Mayor Rudolph W. Giuliani was on foot and walking away from the site, accompanied by Fire Commissioner Thomas Von Essen and Police Commissioner Bernard B. Kerik. All three of the men were caked with dust, and they were moving away from the scene as quickly as possible. Behind them there were also a lot of civilians streaming out of the area... some were walking and others were running. The tension and anxiety in the air was as palpable as the dust. Everyone was determined to get away from the Towers and find a place of safety.

As I approached the World Trade Center site, I was overwhelmed by the sight of debris all over the place. Approximately a foot of dust covered everything, as if some strange snowfall from an alien planet had occurred. The atmosphere was cloudy; a thick haze all around us, and it was extremely difficult to breathe. I now know that air was filled with asbestos, unknowingly affecting so many of us first responders that day.

In the distance I saw the shell of the first Tower. In the time it had taken me to ride the subway, the building had collapsed—but I did not know this yet. My mind refused to acknowledge what my eyes were seeing; telling me it must be some kind of artistic sculpture. My mind wouldn't let me grasp what was happening nor could I begin to comprehend the magnitude of what had already occurred here in the heart of New York City.

As I approached the site, I noticed that there was a lot of paper flying through the air...various sizes of paper and a rainbow of colors kept falling from above. There were also ladies' purses and shoes and other articles of clothing strewn on the ground...an uncommon sight on the streets of Manhattan.

Having lived in the city for years, I had noticed something interesting about the Twin Towers on previous visits to the area. Depending on where you were standing, the Towers sometimes visually appeared to be one single Tower rather than two Towers because they lined up perfectly from certain angles. Consequently, when I got closer, I thought that I was seeing the same optical illusion I had seen so many times before. My brain wasn't acknowledging that one Tower had collapsed. Even with all the debris scattered all over the area, I assumed that one Tower was lined up perfectly behind the other, creating the same optical illusion, and therefore, the image before me appeared to be a single Tower.

Maybe, at that moment, it was a defense mechanism. The buildings were steel and mighty, a testament to the achievements of architecture and man's ingenuity. They could not be felled by a terrorist attack.

I shook my head, as if to bring myself back to the present moment. I needed to determine where the chief who was in charge of the incident might be in all this mess. Locating the chief in charge of a fire or disaster site was usually quite simple, but in this case, it was beyond chaotic and visibility was also impaired by the falling debris and smoke. My intention was to walk over to the water side of the Towers—the West Street side—because I came in from the land side. Then I would report in to the chief and tell him to use me in any way he wanted. I thought he might use me to bring full oxygen cylinders to the guys or just assist in any way that I could. I was there to help so it didn't matter what I might be asked to do.

I slogged through debris and ash, focusing on putting one foot in front of the other as acrid smoke burned at my lungs. As I arrived at Church and Dey Streets, there was more debris of all kinds scattered everywhere. As I continued to shuffle through the chaos, I passed an engine company chauffeur, who is the specially trained driver and operator of the pumper. I got about twenty feet past him, and I heard him ask a civilian to open a hydrant up for him. His request caused me to stop and glance back in his direction.

The civilian was looking at the hydrant wrench and flipping it around. The hydrant wrench is a funny little gadget, and from the way the civilian was handling the wrench, it was apparent that the man didn't know which end was up. So a little small voice told me to go back and open the hydrant up for the chauffeur, which I did. Once I opened the hydrant, I put the hydrant wrench on the engine and made a special point to tell the company chauffeur, "Your wrench is on the rig." You see, hydrant wrenches are very expensive, and if you lose one (which my guys did once and I had to do a lot of paperwork to replace it), it's a big hassle. Among firefighters, the hydrant wrench was closely guarded on the job. None of the officers or firefighters wanted to lose one.

After I put the hydrant wrench on the truck, I looked at the hose line and noticed a cop in a suit holding the nozzle incorrectly. Obviously I am very familiar with firefighting equipment and I knew that if you are not holding a nozzle properly, once the chauffeur charges it with water, you could actually lose control of it and it could whip about.

Once again that little small voice told me to stay here and work with these guys or they were going to get hurt—or hurt people around them, because at this time we were just across the street from the North Tower that was still standing and burning.

We opened the nozzle and began dousing an ambulance that was on fire.

Several firefighters were coming in from home or other firehouses to help. There was so much activity and noise, and it was difficult to identify where the fire chief was or who was giving the orders so at one point I asked one of the firefighters where the staging area was. The "staging area" is the term used for an area located near the command post from where the chief gives direction, including the orders on what floor to attack. When I asked the question, the firefighter looked at me and just shook his head. The expression on his face seemed to say, "Where have you been?" What I didn't realize was that when the South Tower collapsed before I arrived at the scene, the chief and several hundred firefighters were actually dead or still trapped under the rubble.

We were all, in a sense, on our own, yet our humanity linked us together. We worked as a team—helping each other. But it was without a chain of command. Without real guidance. And without a sense of what on earth we were going to do about the North Tower.

As I look back on that historic day, I realize now that I felt a sense of vulnerability and disempowerment while I was at the scene. I asked myself, "How could this have happened in America? Is there no way we can protect Americans from something so unspeakable?" During the years I was on active duty, I always hated it when we were not able to rescue someone from a fire. I would ask myself if there was anything that we could have done differently that could possibly have saved the victim. I'm sure that most firefighters felt the same way that I did at the World Trade Center; we were not able to rescue approximately 3,000 people, including 343 of our comrades from the fire department.

At the writing of this book over ten years have passed, and I still feel such indescribable sadness as I recall the events of that world-changing day. The images of 9/11 still play over and over in my mind at times, and the deafening sounds I heard that day are as real to me today as when they happened.

As I kept working near the North Tower, I tried to assess the situation as accurately as possible. It was difficult to see because of all the smoke, ash, and debris floating through the air. There were also people fleeing the scene as police and fire rescuers continued to arrive. The sights and sounds happening around me were almost too much for my mind to comprehend.

Standing at the base of the North Tower that day at about 10:25 a.m., I remember gazing up at the Tower. There was a huge gaping hole in the side of the building, and smoke was streaming out of the cavernous opening. Memories of the beautiful clear skies and warm sun that had greeted me as I had awakened only hours earlier was more like a dream than the nightmarish reality before me. The skies over the city had quickly transitioned from clear blue to smoke-filled and a gloomy, almost indescribable haze blanketed the entire area around me. As a young Marine in Vietnam, I had seen so much, and suffered severe physical and emotional injuries, but what was about to unfold in the minutes and hours ahead would make my experience in Vietnam pale in comparison because this battle was being fought at home. And the people who died that day were not soldiers. They were civilians. They were moms and dads, brothers and sisters, grandparents and friends. They had left their homes to go to work, to drop off their kids at daycare, to head for a coffee, innocent and unaware that they were about to fall victim to the most outrageous attack on America.

The magnitude of the scene around us was beyond comprehension. There were so many emergency situations to deal with, and a growing but limited number of first responders to handle everything. As a couple of us joined forces to extinguish the flames on the emergency vehicle that was ablaze, I heard a strange sound...it was like a loud pop or a bang. With so much happening in the area, we just kept forging ahead, trying to extinguish the fire. Moments later, the same sound happened, only this time, it was louder and sounded like it was coming from somewhere above us. I don't remember saying anything to the firefighters I was working with. We didn't look up. We just stared at each other as if our gaze was frozen in place. Then the same sound happened again, and somehow we knew that the North Tower was coming down.

Then it happened again...B-A-N-G! Instinct told us that the Tower was collapsing. Now! We started to run, and survival instinct kicked in hard and strong. Each of us knew this was about life or death. As we fled, I don't know if I slipped or tripped over some debris, but in a moment's time I found myself on the ground. As I hit the pavement, a sharp pain shot through my right shoulder. I was in the middle of the street, dust and debris were everywhere. The dust was so thick I was choking. I now couldn't get up on my feet. I slithered along on the hard, dusty surface in a scene out of some vision of hell. I kept trying to get up because I knew from being a firefighter that I needed to get clear of the collapse zone. The facts have been drilled into my brain. The collapse zone is equal to one and a half times the height of a building, and I knew I needed to be at least that far away from the North Tower to be safe. Worse, given the sheer height of the North Tower, that collapse zone was huge.

I quickly realized that my right shoulder was protruding toward the front of my body; from the pain I felt, I knew it had to be dislocated. Still unable to get to my feet, I slid along on my good hand and my knees as the sounds from overhead became deafening. Everything was happening at lightning speed, yet time also seemed to stand still. Then I realized what was happening: the floors of the North Tower were pancaking into each other, and they were picking up momentum as they were collapsing. I knew there was no way that I was clear of the collapse zone. I was, in my mind, going to face my death in the tomb of Ground Zero.

Chapter Three — Life Flashes

We drew strength when our firefighters ran upstairs and risked their lives so that others might live; when rescuers rushed into smoke and fire at the Pentagon; when the men and women of Flight 93 sacrificed themselves to save our nation's Capital; when flags were hanging from front porches all across America, and strangers became friends. It was the worst day we have ever seen, but it brought out the best in all of us.
~John Kerry

Clarence on duty as a firefighter in the FDNY.

The mind is a strange and powerful thing. On my hands and knees with the floors of the North Tower crashing down from above, my mind immediately went to three firefighters we had lost earlier that year on Father's Day. In what seemed like an eternity I thought to myself, "I'm going to die just like those guys did. This wall is going to collapse on me, and I'm not going to make it...I'm going to die."

In seconds, it seemed like my life flashed before my eyes. Bits and pieces of who I was, the life I lived.

New York City had been home for me for some time. I joined the New York City Fire Department in 1978, and retired as a Fire Lieutenant after putting in twenty-two tough but rewarding years with the FDNY. My decision to retire was prompted by a number of things, including the cumulative effects of many life experiences that had greatly impacted my physical and emotional well-being through the years. It started slowly, as one situation built upon another until it was obvious that I had to make a change in my life.

While I was still in high school I enlisted in the U.S. Marine Corps and began my active duty on August 14, 1967 at eighteen years of age during the Vietnam War era. Prior to this time, I faced poverty, segregation, and the Civil Rights movement, attempting to balance these issues with good work ethics and the Christian principles my mother taught me. It was a delicate dance, and one I didn't always balance successfully. Segregation was not only cruel—in many ways it was soul-crushing.

However, in Vietnam, I saw and experienced things that were beyond anything I had ever known in Sumter, South Carolina, where I grew up. After being wounded in the line of duty, I returned to Sumter for a few weeks, and then headed for New York, where my sister lived, to find work. I tried my hand at a number of careers, and eventually became a proud firefighter with the elite few at the New York City Fire Department.

Until the morning of Tuesday, September 11, 2001, my most traumatic life experiences had been my military service on the front lines in Vietnam and the bombing of the World Trade Center in 1993, both of which had a far greater effect on me than I initially understood. The aftermath of the Vietnam War was a dark time in our nation's history, and the incident at the World Trade Center in 1993 represented one of the first attacks that had come to our shores. With these memories etched in my mind, the day-to-day tragedies that I witnessed as a firefighter brought the graphic details of the past back to my mind with heightened awareness. It all finally took a toll on me physically and emotionally, forcing me to retire from the Department. I felt proud to leave on my own terms and in good standing with my fellow firefighters.

However, I've never been a man who can just sit still. Following my retirement from the FDNY, even though I worked hard all my life, I wanted to stay active so I continued on as a mortgage inspector in a part-time job that I began in 1987. The duties involved completing inspections all over New York City and its suburbs, which was easy and also a natural fit for me. My years of experience as a firefighter had familiarized me with the layout of the city, and this made my work as a mortgage inspector very easy to execute. I would get the inspection assignments on the first of the month, and I had until the end of the month to complete them.

After my retirement, I was also looking for a fire safety director's job in an office building in Manhattan, even though I was still doing mortgage inspections on a part-time basis. Several of the places that I applied to said I was overqualified, adding that they wouldn't hire me because I would have been coming on the job as a retired Fire Lieutenant, which warranted a higher rate of pay, but I didn't give up.

One day I finally landed a fire safety director's job after several failed attempts of employment at other companies. I was in an office doing an inspection, and I mentioned to the office manager that I had been looking for a fire safety director's job in a building like this.

He said, "Are you still looking?"

I responded with a resounding, "Yes."

Basically, he hired me on the spot. The company had an agency that handled the hiring, firing, and management of the building, so he gave me their number. I called them and made an appointment for an interview. When I met with them I told them how much I wanted regarding my salary. The agent told me, "I don't think they're going to give that to you." But the office manager said, "Hire him," and they did.

The agency hired me on September 7, 2001, the Friday before 9/11. When I left there that Friday afternoon, I was so happy that I had gotten the job that my excitement was probably evident to everyone I passed on the street. I was walking down the sidewalk laughing, and jumping up, practically clicking my feet together. I was looking forward to starting my new position the following Thursday. I always like a new challenge to conquer, and I knew it was a job where I could excel.

How life can change in the blink of an eye.

As I woke up that Tuesday morning on September 11, 2001, I was excited about the challenges ahead of me. I had already planned out my day, organized the forms I needed, and mapped out my route the night before, which included completing several mortgage inspections all over Brooklyn that day...just like any other day. Little did I know how quickly my carefully planned day would change the rest of my life.

Time stood still momentarily as the sounds of the collapsing Tower triggered vivid memories of rescue efforts in the past. In those moments as I fled for safety I had flashbacks of Vietnam as well as from the first bombing of the World Trade Center in 1993. As these memories flashed through my mind, it was as if I was back in Vietnam...then I was at the World Trade Center bombing... then I was back at the base of the North Tower, running for my life.

I just kept running away from the collapsing building, hoping I had enough time to get out of the way. Because before I could even think about helping anyone else, I had to make sure I got to safety. And then, of course, I'd been slammed to the ground; my should dislocated. In a haze of dust. My own personal tomb.

The words, "I'm going to die," began to echo over and over in my mind. "I'm going to die just like those three guys did...the wall of this building is going to collapse on me and I'm going to die..."

There I was on my hands and knees...just waiting for the inevitable to happen. During those paralyzing seconds, it was surprisingly very peaceful. I was ready to go. In that final moment I knew I was ready to go home to meet my Lord as death came to claim me.

I know that sounds strange. Even as I write the words, I find it hard to believe I was that calm in the moment. But I was.

Maybe it was because I'd been close to death so many times because it came with the territory—in Vietnam, as a firefighter, during the previous bombing of the Towers. When death is a companion, you have to make peace with it somehow. My faith and courage enabled me to do that.

Time seemed to stop once again as the sounds of the collapsing Tower came to a halt. Still on my hands and knees, I began to move my body as I finally realized that I had survived the collapse somehow. Unable to do so just seconds before, I eased my way up off the ground.

As soon as I stood up, I became very aware of the dust cloud that hung over the area. The haze was incredibly thick, and it was so difficult to breathe that every breath was suffocating. The space around me was totally saturated with grey powder. Even though it was midmorning, it was as dark as night. I felt like I was on another planet. I was not of this world. If I didn't know any better, I might have actually assumed I was dead. But the burning feeling in my throat and the agonizing pain in my shoulder sharply reminded me. I was alive. The pain kept me alert and aware.

By some miracle I was still alive.

Seemingly alone in the gloomy darkness and intensely aware of the thick dust, I started talking to myself.

"What are you going to do now, Clarence?" I asked.

I couldn't see anyone or anything so I just kept talking to myself. It helped to ground me and keep me focused in the craziness.

"Just breathe shallow like you would if you were fighting a fire in a smoke-filled building."

I started breathing shallow and began to apply the techniques I had used as a firefighter so many times. Unable to see anything, and feeling as if I was blind, I extended my left arm because the other was throbbing with pain. With one arm jutting out in front of me to avoid colliding with anything that might be in my pathway, I slowly made my way back to join the living. The dust was so thick that I couldn't even see my hand in front of my face. That moment was the closest thing I have ever experienced to being blind, and it was a feeling of total helplessness.

I felt extreme pain, but I was grateful for it because it let me know that I was still alive.

Chapter Four - A Survivor's Story

And I pray they will be comforted by a power greater than any of us, spoken through the ages in Psalm 23:
"Even though I walk through the valley of the shadow of death, I fear no evil, for You are with me."
~President George W. Bush, September 11, 2001.

The debris from 9/11 covers a rescue truck.

I kept talking to myself as I tried to get oriented, saying, "Walk away from the incident," which I started to do. Now that I was on my feet again, I started using the walk that I had used so many times as a firefighter.

It's amazing, really, how the mind works. When I was trained as a Marine, I knew the training was designed so that those skills became "second nature." When you are under artillery fire, there isn't time to think. Training in the fire department and the police department are based on that same concept. In a heavy fire, with flames all around, a firefighter must use instinct—the training must be, literally, a part of him or her. There's not time to think—you must act quickly and decisively. It could be a matter of life and death. And it often is.

That day, 9/11, was no different. I couldn't see anything so I kept my weight on my back foot as I probed with the forward foot to make sure I wasn't falling in any holes or anything else that might be strewn in the street. I wonder how many people without my training were injured that day. Or perhaps even died.

I was moving methodically along when I came in contact with a brick wall that seemed to be about six feet tall, gauging from my own height, which is five feet, eleven inches. Since I only had one good arm due to the apparent shoulder dislocation, I wasn't able to scale the wall. I remember backing up a little bit and turning to my left, where I encountered another wall that was masked by the thick dust that saturated the air. Fortunately, this wall was a little shorter so even with my bad arm, my chances of getting over this obstacle were significantly improved. With as much speed as I could muster, I managed to put my good arm over first and pull myself up. Then, assisting as much as I could with the arm that was dislocated, I eased my way up and over, agony shooting through my body.

Once I got over the wall, I remember walking down three steps where I saw the fire marshal that I was working with earlier—at least, I thought I did. I was surprised to see him standing there, and he didn't have a speck of dust on him. Dust at this time was so prevalent that it seemed like it was going around corners...there was no way to escape the volume of dust that was everywhere. I paused for just a moment and looked at him, thinking, "He doesn't have any dust on him. I should have run to wherever he ran."

I noticed that he was standing near a doorway, and the door was one of those glass doors with a bar that you push when you are on the inside so you can exit the building. There appeared to be a great deal of light shining in through this door.

The fire marshal looked at me and said, "I see you made it."

I didn't realize it at the time, but his words were words of encouragement to me.

I said, "Yeah, you too."

I asked him for my camera—earlier, we had been snapping pictures because we knew we were literally a part of history. I wanted my own children to "never forget," as they say. I am sure he was motivated for those same reasons. We needed to preserve what was happening there at Ground Zero.

He felt in the pocket of his turnout coat and replied, "I dropped it; I was running for my life."

"Me too, no problem," I said as I left him and kept moving.

Almost immediately four or five EMS guys came into view. They were walking my way, and they were covered with a thick layer of dust from head to toe. It was as if we were all one race; we all looked the same, panic-stricken people covered head to toe with gray ash. Each of the rescue workers had a handkerchief tied around their mouths to help them breathe as well as to prevent the dust from going into their lungs. They gestured in my direction and shouted to one another, "There's no one over there that needs assistance."

I yelled back to them, "Hey guys, I'm injured; I need help."

In response to my desperate plea, they ran over toward me as quickly as they could, carefully navigating through the debris that was all over the ground. One guy maneuvered his way around me on one side. Not knowing what kind of injuries I had, he grabbed my injured arm, and immediately I yelled, "*That's* the arm that's injured!" Wow, that burst of pain really snapped me into the present!

He adjusted his grip and grabbed me in a better spot. Someone helped on the other side of me, and together they lifted me onto the gurney and started moving away from the area toward the ambulance. Even though it was mid-morning, the dust in the air made it so dark that it was visually impossible to know where you were. It was as if the sun had set and we had been plunged into darkness. I would imagine the experience was much like

Hiroshima or Nagasaki in that regard. In fact, moments later we came to a street corner, and one of the EMS guys had to shine his flashlight up at the street sign to determine where we were.

In addition to the poor visibility, everywhere the eye could see was littered with dust and debris. This made it very difficult for the EMS guys to move the gurney toward their nearby ambulance that they were going to use to transport me out of the chaos and hell near the North Tower—or where the North Tower once stood. At one point I remember one of the EMS guys asking me if I could walk. I was so exhausted and didn't realize at the time, but I was traumatized because I didn't even answer him. I was in shock. When I didn't respond, they continued rolling the gurney toward the ambulance, which we firefighters and police officers refer to as "the bus."

Once I was in the bus I remember being in excruciating pain because of my dislocated shoulder. I was also beginning to experience "survivor's guilt" because I had gone to the scene to help out—and now rescue personnel had to assist me. Being a retired Fire Lieutenant I knew that once a person is injured, other people have to be taken off the line to assist you. However, a rescuer at heart, I didn't want to be the one responsible for taking others away from the scene. I had gone to help out, but ended up needed assistance. And of course, at that time, I had no idea yet just how many people had perished when the Towers fell.

On the way to the hospital, the ambulance picked up other civilians who also needed help. Since they were helping other people too, this somewhat eased my overwhelming feelings of guilt. As the driver navigated carefully through the dust and debris, I begged the young EMS lady who was in the back of the bus with us to snap my shoulder back in place to ease the pain. However, the woman quietly said, "No, I can't do it. We have to take you to the hospital."

We finally arrived at St. Vincent's. As the ambulance pulled up to the emergency entrance, there were medical personnel including doctors and nurses standing outside of the hospital. I eventually learned that the doctors and nurses were standing there because they had anticipated a large influx of people coming in to be treated. However, the volume of people anticipated by the medical personnel at St. Vincent's never became a reality because most of the people died during the collapse. Again, at the time, we just had no way of knowing what this awful day would mean when the dead were finally tallied—let alone all of those who survived and the psychological toll that day took.

Meanwhile, the EMS guys took me into the emergency room. There were a couple of doctors there and some nurses as well. One of the emergency room doctors looked at me and said, "You know that the proper way to do this is to give you anesthesia to render you unconscious, and then we can reset your arm. We're expecting a lot of people to come in, so we can do one of two things: we can reset your arm the proper way, but it could take a long time because you would have to wait...or we could just snap it back into place without any anesthesia."

After all of the things I've been through, of course I said, "Snap it back into place, Doc!"

And the doctor obliged—not without a scream from me—despite thinking of myself as a strong guy!

After my shoulder was back in place, the doctor pointed toward the corner and told me that there was a sink that I could wash the dust off of me. I had been aware of the dust related to my breathing, but I had not even thought about the possibility that I might be covered with dust. While I saw all of the others covered with the grayness, it didn't dawn on me that I was just like them. I didn't realize how much dust was on my face and my entire body until I actually saw myself in the centerfold of *Life Magazine* some time later. The picture showed me as an almost unrecognizable person on the hospital gurney covered in a thick, suffocating, poisonous fine powder.

Before leaving the emergency room, the doctor made me promise that I would go for follow-up treatment because my arm needed to be looked at as soon as possible by a professional.

I promised that I would go get medical attention as soon as this mayhem eased up a little. Of course at that time, it seemed like it had gone on forever, and would never end.

At the writing of this book over ten years have passed since my shoulder was injured as the North Tower collapsed. I don't understand why, but since that day, whenever I talk about the World Trade Center and what happened on 9/11, my right shoulder begins to hurt. I don't understand this phenomenon, yet every time I talk about the Twin Towers or the World Trade Center, I begin rubbing my right shoulder because it starts to hurt. I remember asking my therapist about it once in hopes of better understanding what prompts the unexplainable pain in my shoulder.

It still amazes me that it's apparently related to the extreme trauma I experienced. I can't really explain it, but it's something that I'm aware of now. It still happens...even when I'm in group therapy.

So, I took myself and my injured shoulder that day, and exited the hospital. While being treated at St. Vincent's Hospital, the doctor had cut my T-shirt off, which had the fire department "FDNY" logo on the back and the Maltese cross logo on the front. Consequently, when I left the hospital after my shoulder had been "treated" by popping it back into place, I was wearing my dust-covered jeans, a hospital gown, which was wrapped around me, and my arm had been temporarily immobilized in a sling. It was still fairly early in the morning, and some of the stores either weren't open yet or had chosen not to open or most likely they couldn't open because of what was going on in the area around the World Trade Center. Whatever the reason, I needed to buy a shirt so I could dispose of the hospital gown.

As I was walking down the street, it must have been evident to some people that I had been at the World Trade Center site. As I made my way along the street, two young men from England with strong accents came over to me, and we started talking. We walked along together; talking about what was happening and what had occurred until we finally found a store that was open. The two guys went into the shop, and after a few minutes returned with a new T-shirt, which they had purchased for me. I thanked them and put the shirt on as quickly as my aching shoulder would tolerate.

Once I left the two kind gentlemen who bought the T-shirt for me, I discovered that there wasn't any public transportation heading back downtown. Everything was at a standstill, but I was determined to go back down to the World Trade Center site, though. I'm hard-wired that way. If I could help in any way, I was going to.

I walked the distance to Ground Zero. Just before I got to the area, I pulled my lieutenant's badge out of my pocket and pinned it on my newly acquired T-shirt, anticipating that there would be security in the area. At the time, I had no real sense of how the landscape of Lower Manhattan had been changed. Forever.

Chapter Five — Leaving Ground Zero

Love and compassion are necessities, not luxuries.
Without them humanity cannot survive.
~*The Dalai Lama*

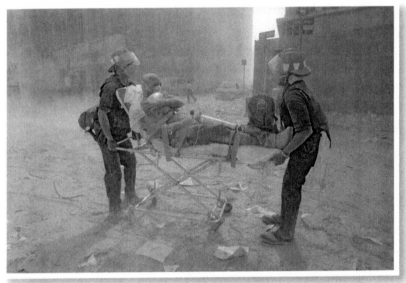

Clarence on a stretcher after the towers collapse on 9/11/01.

I kept walking until I arrived back at the scene of the disaster. I met up with a company of firefighters, and I just stayed with them for a while because duty was still calling me. Standing there...face to face with the remnants of what had once been the iconic Twin Towers of the New York skyline...I felt compelled to help.

There was also a cop there in the immediate area who noticed my arm in a sling. He asked me why I didn't leave because there were fresh firefighters and police officers coming in. I don't remember if I responded to his question or not. I just stayed for a while, staring at the massive mound of rubble, hoping that there were survivors beneath the twisted metal. The images of the collapsed Towers were just too much to comprehend, and the prospect of so many lost lives on American soil was more than my mind could take in.

I have since talked to people who watched the day unfold from television sets around the country. They echo my feeling. It was as if, despite the rubble, despite the gaping hole in the ground, we could not possibly process that all those angels ascended to heaven that day. There *had* to be pockets of survivors.

As a person in the rescue "business," so to speak, I thought of earthquakes I had seen on the news—places like San Francisco and Japan—where even days later, survivors had been found.

I was certain this was going to be true here. At Ground Zero.

After staying at the scene for a while I finally realized that I was useless because at this point I only had one good arm so I started walking away from the scene. My intention was to walk across the Brooklyn Bridge and back into Brooklyn. As I headed in that direction, I saw a fire department van so I flagged the driver down, and he gave me a ride across the bridge.

During the hours after the collapse, I knew my sons in North Carolina and my friend, MaryAnn, were calling me because my phone kept ringing intermittently. I realized they were probably worrying about me because they had heard that the second Tower had collapsed, and they were aware that I had gone down to the scene. However, every time I attempted to answer my phone, the call would drop and I would lose the signal. I learned later that this was because of the volume of calls being made by all those who had been injured or were still in the area. With so many people trying to reach their loved ones or call for help, they were overloading the circuits of the cell phone service providers. Across the globe, people were unable to reach their friends in New York City, and no doubt many tears of worry were shed, many prayers were offered up. For some, those prayers would remain unanswered in the way they hoped.

My own family, meanwhile, had no idea if I was dead or alive.

After crossing the Brooklyn Bridge, I got out of the fire department van and got on the train. I still had dust on me and my arm hung limp in the sling. I rode the subway until I reached the station where I had parked my car. About that time I realized that it was almost time for MaryAnn to be getting off work. Rather than heading for my apartment, I headed toward the high school where she worked to give her a ride before I went home to clean up.

As soon as I was a bit clear of downtown, I was again able to use my phone. The first person I called was my son Cody; I knew he was worried about me. Because he had begged me not to go over to the site earlier, I made sure that I called him to put his mind at ease and I told him to tell Clarence Jevon that I was injured but alive. I was feeling kind of distraught as I told him on the phone, "You know, I went over to help out, and now I am injured."

He reassured me that I had done some good at the site, adding, "You did the best that you could do, and things worked out the way that they were supposed to." I agreed with him, but I still felt grief tugging at the corners of my heart.

I continued on my way to MaryAnn's workplace. She shed tears at the sight of me. But we were both grateful for the miracle of my survival. A few feet closer to the collapse zone, and I would not have survived. It's still surreal to me all these years later.

After I picked her up, we went back to my apartment where I showered off the dust of Ground Zero, put on one of my blue fire department shirts, a fresh pair of jeans, and shoes before going back to the hospital for the treatment I had promised to get after I left the emergency room at St. Vincent's.

Although my arm was in a sling, the pain was starting to increase by this time. It didn't classify as excruciating pain—not the way it had when it was dislocated—but it was very painful. As my friend and I walked into the emergency room, there was a doctor there who was on his way home. However, when he saw me, he came back to help me out.

He said, "I can tell that you were at the World Trade Center because everyone that came to the hospital from the site has red eyes like yours." He sent me for x-rays and gave me a prescription for medication. When I hesitated regarding the prescription—I was always a little leery of pain pills—the technician looked at me and said, "No, you go to the pharmacy and have this filled as soon as possible because you're going to need it."

When I reflect back on that day, I need to offer a note of thanks to all those people in the medical field. I was treated with such compassion and kindness and care that day. I think we all felt so *helpless,* that we treated each other with *extra* care, as if to somehow make up for the losses of that day.

By this time it was late, but I knew of a twenty-four-hour drugstore in Brooklyn, so I went and had the prescription filled as instructed. And I must admit that I'm glad that I did because that night I was in such terrible, excruciating pain that I wasn't able to sleep. Although I didn't realize it at the time, I know I was also traumatized just thinking about what had happened at the Twin Towers. My mind was racing, and the events of the day kept replaying over and over in my mind. I couldn't get those graphic images out of my head. Unfortunately, this would continue for some time.

Chapter Six – Dark Days and Nights

Depression is nourished by a lifetime of ungrieved and
unforgiven hurts.
~*Penelope Sweet*

9/11 ceremony in Annapolis, MD in 2010.

In the days that followed 9/11, as a nation we were plunged into
a dark grief. Day after day there was coverage of the funerals of
hundreds and indeed, thousands, of people. By now, of course,
I knew a plane had crashed in Pennsylvania, and that people had
perished at the Pentagon. It seemed as if death was all around us.

I was fortunate to have MaryAnn as a friend during this time
because I was an emotional wreck and unable to take care of myself.
After I was injured in the collapse, I could eat, but I was depressed
and didn't have the emotional energy to prepare the food. To help

me through this difficult time, my friend would go to work, return to her home after work, prepare meals for me, and bring them to my apartment. During the daytime, all I would do was lie in bed and hide in the darkness. I didn't want any sunlight to come in and remind me that another day had begun.

Before the World Trade Center incident, I loved the sunshine and would never think of covering my windows. However, after 9/11 I wanted to just sleep and forget what had happened. I drew the blinds shut tight.

I craved the darkness.

And yet I could not sleep.

In addition to my struggle with depression, sleep was elusive because of the excruciating pain associated with my shoulder injury. At times I would just sit on the side of the bed and watch the news and all the footage about the collapse of the Towers. I was drawn to it, as if somehow, if I watched enough coverage, I would be able to make sense of something that, to this day, is unfathomable.

In addition to the physical pain, I was trying to deal with some deep emotional pain. The events of 9/11 triggered old memories from Vietnam and the trauma that I experienced when I fought there as a young Marine. I didn't want to go to sleep because my dreams began to haunt me. They were horrible dreams, which sometimes combined all the things that had traumatized me in life. I would have dreams about a building collapsing on me... explosions and gunfire...airplanes crashing... bayonets...death and destruction.

Despite my faith, I traveled to a dark, dark place.

When I returned from Vietnam I was afraid to go to sleep at night because of the nightmares and horrible dreams I was having. Now more than thirty years later, all of those dreams were back, and they were compounded by the sights and sounds I experienced during the devastating collapse on 9/11.

Despite my daily struggles and the emotional ups and downs, on a number of occasions, I found enough courage to walk to the store by myself. Each time I ventured out, I had a difficult time doing that and just couldn't wait to get back home and get back into bed. That's the way I lived for several months. I only felt safe in my own apartment.

And before I knew it, my apartment had become my prison.

MaryAnn was a social worker professionally and was very concerned about me. She knew that I was suffering, but she didn't really have a clue about how to help me come out of the depression and post-traumatic stress that I was experiencing.

Even though I suffered with deep depression and was not easy to be around, MaryAnn was such a good friend to me during the weeks and months after 9/11. She helped me through some really rough times. Looking back on that period, I don't know what I would have done without her.

In addition to MaryAnn, others also reached out to me in their own ways. My daughter, Tonia, called several times a week to see how I was doing. After I was injured at the site, some days I would come home and find dozens of messages on my voicemail from friends who were concerned about me and had called to see how I was doing.

There is one fellow in my neighborhood—I don't know his name, but whenever he saw me, he yelled out, "Hello, hero!" We didn't know each other by name, but we lived in the same subdivision. Whenever he saw me wearing any of my fire department paraphernalia like a sweatshirt with the firefighter emblem on it, he never failed to greet me. And it always made me smile.

We had hardly ever spoken to one another, but I think he was an EMT because one of his vehicles had the EMT logo on it. I think that's the connection, and the bonding had come about because we had done the same type of work. It was always nice to see him wave at me when I passed, and it was really gratifying to know that people cared. I appreciated, too, that perhaps he understood me a little. While my family *loved* me, I know they could not walk in my shoes, and of course I didn't want them to. I wanted to shield everyone from the horrors I had experienced. They hadn't seen the Tower fall from my vantage point. They hadn't seen the rice paddies of Vietnam. They could try to understand, but in some ways, I felt terribly, terribly alone.

I did learn some very simple, but very important life lessons through all of that. It may sound corny, but I learned to never, ever underestimate how valuable acts of kindness and a few well-chosen words of encouragement are to friends and neighbors. Whenever one of your friends goes through a hard time or difficult circumstances, I encourage you to take a few minutes to pick up the phone and let them know that you're thinking of them. I can tell you from personal experience that it really makes a difference. It's such as simple, gentle gesture, but to someone in need it can mean the world.

For some people, it may be a literal lifeline.

As time passed, the city—and all of us first responders—tried to move on. It was hard to believe that I had gone from being on cloud nine right before 9/11 when I had gotten a great job and was so excited about my future, to being closed up inside hiding from the world. I kept trying to think back to that moment, when I was walking down the sidewalk so happy and excited about what was to come. If I tried hard enough, maybe I could get that feeling back, remember what it was like to feel good, to feel special. But no matter how hard I tried, after the collapse and horrific events of Tuesday, September 11, 2001, each day brought an unexplainable but deepening sadness to my heart.

Fortunately, my job was still there for me, and I did do well at it, but for some reason it became such a challenge for me to get dressed and go to work. I felt sad all the time, and I didn't understand why. I was so depressed and heavy-hearted that I didn't know at the time that I was suffering from trauma and post traumatic stress related to everything I saw and experienced on 9/11 and in Vietnam. I was working at a good job, I was alive after such a horrific event, yet I couldn't feel happy again. It was very frustrating for a guy like me.

I like to think I can handle anything, but it was obvious that some things are much bigger than me.

I was still working part-time at my mortgage inspection job at this time, so I took the night tour from 11:00 p.m.-7:00 a.m. in my position as a fire safety director. Because of my responsibilities at my new job, I missed my follow-up appointment with the doctor regarding my shoulder. This also delayed my corrective surgery. I didn't realize I was falling down the proverbial rabbit hole. It was a domino effect, and I wasn't taking care of myself like I knew I should. I had been trained to stay in shape and to stay healthy, but that was before the tragedy.

As part of my daily routine, I would usually drop by my old firehouse—Ladder 12— when I would get off work in the mornings after inspecting various office buildings in Manhattan. The first day I stopped by shortly after the collapse of the Tower, a couple of guys were standing outside. One of the firefighters came up to me, put his arms around me, and fell into my arms crying. It was a very sad situation because we lost several guys from our firehouse, including the chief and his aide, who was a good friend of mine. He didn't serve in Vietnam, but he was a Vietnam buff, and we often spent time discussing the Vietnam War. It was tough to face everyone because it was a constant reminder of the losses we experienced that day.

At the firehouse when you walked into the kitchen, the tables were full of food that had been brought in by people from the community as an expression of their support. There was a memorial set up in front of the firehouse honoring the guys that had died from the company. Only two out of eight of our guys made it out of the Twin Towers alive that day. One of them stayed around the firehouse for several weeks after the collapse. When he first came back from Ground Zero, they had to cut his boots off his feet. He was so traumatized that he was unable to go home, so he slept, ate, showered, and changed clothes in the firehouse. It became something of a work prison to him, where he was a voluntary inmate.

Still, I kept on working, maybe because I didn't know what else to do. Because I continued to delay my shoulder surgery, getting dressed for work was a real chore. The sharp pain was a daily reminder of something I tried to forget.

Getting to work was another challenge. I had a metro card that I used in the city to take the subway. You gain access to the train by putting the card in the turnstile, which reads the card and grants you admission. During those days, my arm was in such bad condition that I found it very difficult to even reach into my pocket for the card. That's how bad my arm had gotten.

Because of my work schedule, after being injured on September 11, it wasn't until October 28 that I actually got around to having the surgery on my shoulder. The surgery I had promised that doctor that I would get right away.

The procedure was performed on an outpatient surgery basis at the hospital. I can remember them putting me under the anesthesia, with no other memories from the operation until I woke up with a start. When the surgery was done, and I came out of the anesthetic, I remember being in the emergency room, where it was very cold. They still hadn't put covers over me from the surgery, so I woke up freezing. I vaguely remember one of the medical personnel kindly covering me with comforting blankets as I drifted in and out of consciousness. The next thing I remember, the nurse was gently shaking me out of my slumber.

"Who wants to wake up?" I thought. "I just want to sleep forever." The depression had a hold on me as tight as anything I had ever experienced. I have learned that one trauma can easily cause another to resurface, which I'm sure is what had happened to me. It was undeniable. This trauma brought back all the stuff that happened in that other chaotic situation—Vietnam, not to mention the World Trade Center bombing in 1993.

After the surgery, my friend MaryAnn once again came to my rescue, picked me up, and took me back to my apartment. She stayed around for a while to make sure I was comfortable, but finally had to leave because of her responsibilities at her own home.

I was always by myself at night. I was alone. All alone. I remember one night I couldn't sleep after my surgery so with nothing to do, I sat on the side of my bed and ate about forty soft-baked cookies as I watched scenes from the Twin Towers tragedy play over and over on my TV. I didn't realize how much pain these images brought to me. I thought I could handle it, but I didn't comprehend the depth of the suffering that was taking place deep down inside me.

After my operation, I began regular physical therapy sessions shortly to start the process of restoring the movement to my shoulder. During this time, I always had great difficulty leaving the house because I just couldn't shake those feelings of sadness and depression. On a few occasions if I really needed something I tried to go to the corner store and even that was often too much for me, physically and emotionally. So most of the time, the only reason I would leave the house was to go to physical therapy. I reported for therapy three times a week at the hospital. The sessions were intended to break up the scar tissue from the surgery and prevent my shoulder from locking in place. Those hours of rehabilitation were more difficult than I ever imagined, and the pain was astounding. However, despite all of those challenges, little by little I started to regain mobility to my shoulder.

When I first started physical therapy, I couldn't extend my arm more than a few inches from my side, but gradually over days and weeks, the physical therapist got it so I could elevate it a little more. I still don't have full use of my arm even today. It continues to bother me, and the doctors have told me that it will only get worse, but life goes on. I'm still here!

I found out later on during my physical therapy treatments that my insurance had run out some time earlier, and all I was doing was paying the $10 copayment. The ladies in physical therapy continued to treat me without notifying me that my insurance had run out. Their kindness and generosity toward me meant so much that I was overwhelmed when I found out. This was just one of many acts of kindness that were shown to me during this time of my life. After seeing the effects of destruction that man can cause,

I welcomed the glimpses of generosity, of human spirit. It helped give me the hope and strength to go on.

During one of my trips to physical therapy, I noticed some of the signs at the bus stop, which caught my attention. The message of the signs basically said if you need help with depression and post-traumatic stress that you endured from the 9/11 tragedy that you should go see a therapist. I thought about this every time I read those signs. I stared at them and memorized every inch of those posters. I wasn't sure how it would happen, but I knew in my heart that I needed some help.

Then, at some point, the New York City Police Department ordered all of their guys to go to therapy. When I found this out, I felt like it all made sense. Like it was meant to happen this way. Maybe I wasn't falling into the dark abyss. Maybe I was going to get better. With the department's urging, it made it easier for me to seek the help I desperately needed. I went to the VA Hospital in Brooklyn, and I signed up for group therapy. I had been a tough guy my whole life.

Maybe for once I was the one who needed to be rescued.

Chapter Seven — Hope

The greatest of all miracles is to be alive.
~*Thich Nhat Hanh*

Working in the FDNY during a cold winter.

In the midst of the darkness, I innately understood I needed to find the bits of faith and hope to hold on to. Like a drowning man, I needed little signs of hope and goodness in a world gone mad, a world where evil men could hijack a plane and crash it into a building.

One thing that stood out to me was that during the time of my injury and following my surgery, I wasn't able to pay my bills or anything like that. I was too paralyzed by my grief and depression. I was dragging myself to my job but mostly wandering around as if I was sleepwalking. Truly, my memories of that time are hazy.

Finally, I called my creditors. I told them my story, and amazingly all of them understood. I think I went two or three months without paying my monthly bills until I was finally well enough to resume that. It wasn't that I didn't have the money, it just seemed so unimportant. I just felt like it didn't matter. After what I had seen, what was the difference if I did or didn't pay for electricity? Once I got things into perspective, it just amazed me how everyone understood after I told them who I was and what had happened with me. There was no problem; it didn't go to a credit agency or become delinquent. They just basically put everything on hold. Maybe it seems like a small thing, but it was another act of kindness that started to restore a little of my faith in humanity.

Another thing that happened was that along with the darkness of post-9/11 times, there was also light. The yin and yang.

America united during this time. It reminded me of my time in the service, because everyone in the company that I was with all got along very well. We were away from homes and families, and we took care of each other. Of course there was the occasional squabbling, but we all realized that at that moment, we had to count on each other. You know the expression, "There's no 'I' in TEAM"? In Vietnam, we all understood that we relied on each other for support and stability.

America, post-9/11, seemed to have much the same mentality. I remember reading an interview with the actress Sharon Stone after 9/11. She said that post-9/11, she made a point of introducing herself to the person seated next to her on a plane because you never know if you will need to help each other in a crisis, like those on the Flight 93. Their heroic actions—like a platoon in Vietnam, working together—helped bring that plane down in an isolated area of Pennsylvania as opposed to a more populous area. They died together so that others could live. That kind of courage is inspiring. So America seemed to be waking up and realizing we are stronger together than divided by our petty differences or things like race and religion and political beliefs.

In the aftermath of 9/11, patriotism was at an all-time high. American flags were being flown everywhere. We were proud to be Americans, unlike the anti-American sentiments I had experienced during the Vietnam-era protests.

Faith united us as well.

Church pews were filled with people searching for answers. America began to pull together as "one nation...under God... indivisible, with liberty and justice for all."

We couldn't fully understand this tragedy. We, as human beings, with our limited insights, could not comprehend. So we were turning, in record numbers, to something greater than ourselves.

It didn't take long for the level of patriotism to return to where it had been before the collapse. Things changed after 9/11 just as they had after we returned from Vietnam. The old routine slowly edged its way back into people's lives as kindness, respect, and unity began to evaporate from the hearts of the people.

But for a shining moment, it was the hope we wanted and it was certainly the hope I desperately needed.

Chapter Eight – Moving Forward

Courage is the ladder on which all other virtues mount.
~*Clare Boothe Luce*

Clarence is recognized at a flag ceremony.

S hortly after the collapse, I was asked to come over to the Ground Zero site to do an interview for a TV show. That morning I got dressed in my Lieutenant's dress blue uniform and arrived in plenty of time to do the interview. It was a really good thing, the way that it all happened. The newswoman introduced herself and started talking to me about my experiences on that fateful day. As we talked, I noticed the cameraman nearby, and he was filming. I thought it was a practice shot, so when it was over I expected to go back and do the live interview. However, I learned that what I thought was just a trial run was actually the interview for the program. Since it was over so quickly, I didn't even have a chance to get nervous or anxious. It was another small step for me as I tried to regain a life of normalcy.

I brought a couple of photos with me that day, as well as the *Life Magazine* that I was featured in. Several people that were there visiting the site asked to see the photos. There was a large group of tourists there, and some asked me if I wanted to sell the pictures of myself where I was on the hospital gurney. I immediately declined because while I understood that they wanted something tangible from that day, I wasn't ready to be a symbol of that. After all, I only responded on 9/11 because duty called and something deep within urged me to go. I guess it was like my current wife once told me, "You have the heart of a hero."

Following the interview, I gave a lot of autographs to the spectators who had gathered around to watch the production crew film the TV show. They kept asking questions about what it was like, and how I was doing. Some of them were from other countries, and in retrospect I imagine that I was one of the only people that was at the collapse that they had encountered. So I didn't really mind. I stayed as long as necessary to sign for each person who asked. It felt good to help share some reality with them about that day. Instead of watching the same images over and over, I tried to tell them what actually happened and how it felt. I think as a nation—and as I realized from some of the foreigners there that day, as a global community—we are still struggling to make sense of the events. Despite that brief encounter with a glimpse of "fame," I quickly remembered that my day to day reality was far more complex.

Immediately following 9/11, New Yorkers dealt with all kinds of stress on various levels. My issues involved feelings related to my personal experiences at Ground Zero. Days and weeks after the collapse, I felt confused at times and couldn't really comprehend all that had happened. There were moments when I would ask my friends, "Am I dead or alive?" Everything was surreal, and it seemed as if I should have been killed because of my proximity to the collapse. I thought, "Since I have never been dead before, I don't know how it would feel. Could being dead still feel as if I was alive?"

Each time I would pose a question like this, my friends would reassure me by saying, "Clarence, you are alive, and we're here for you."

I lived in an apartment on the eighth floor of a fifteen-story building on Ocean Avenue in Brooklyn. Shortly after the collapse of the Towers, on several occasions when I would be walking up to the apartment building, I would look at it from across the street and have reservations about going in. I had some apprehension about going home. I had the unmistakable feeling that this building too was going to collapse.

One morning, I was lying in bed, and I actually felt the building vibrate. I brushed it off as my imagination playing tricks on me. I needed to get ahold of myself, but over a period of time I felt it again. This time, I went downstairs to the manager's office in the lobby of the building and told them what I was experiencing. The manager said they hadn't gotten a report from anyone else. At one point, they even called the fire department to check it out, and to pacify me and my irrational claims. I knew one of the chiefs personally that showed up. He was a firefighter that I had worked with when I was active in the FDNY, but they searched and couldn't find anything. The building department was also called out, and they assured us that there was no reason for the building to be shaking either.

Some time later, one of the other tenants told me that she had felt the shaking also. Whether the movement was just the building settling or something more, I was so relieved to know that I wasn't totally imagining things because of the tragedy of 9/11. That lady could have just been appeasing me, but it did make me feel like maybe I wasn't totally losing it.

A number of support groups were formed by the Red Cross in the weeks and months after the collapse of the Twin Towers for victims of the World Trade Center attack. I joined several support groups and started attending with a vengeance. As a matter of fact, at one point my therapist at the military base stopped me from attending so many groups. She told me it wasn't good for me to keep searching and bouncing from group to group. Of course she was right, and I took her advice and settled on two groups: one with my therapist and one organized through the Red Cross. I was just so desperate to be back to my old self. To be normal again.

I had a strange experience one evening as I arrived early in Manhattan at the Red Cross meeting. I was standing outside before the meeting was to begin when I realized that I had trouble standing next to the building. The group meeting organized by the Red Cross was held in a tall building, approximately fifty stories high. I was standing under a veranda, and suddenly it seemed as if it was going to fall on me.

On another occasion I was standing outside of the building waiting for the meeting to start. I was looking around at the people on the streets and for whatever reason, I suddenly imagined them as being World Trade Center victims, that is, people having to jump from the upper floors to their death, and it left me with a sense of hopelessness and despair.

I know I was just one of many who suffered from the trauma of everything that happened on 9/11. I've also heard stories that there were veterans from Vietnam who were walking around the rubble at the scene, and all they were saying was their name, rank, and serial number. It's common knowledge in the military that if you are captured during a war, you only give the enemy the very basic information, and that's what these veterans were doing.

As a rule I didn't talk much at the Red Cross group meetings about the collapse and what I experienced there. On a few occasions,

I spoke up, but didn't really express my feelings a lot. Much later I discovered that one of the symptoms of post-traumatic stress is not being willing or able to talk about the ordeal. Since then I have learned that talking about a trauma or a traumatic experience can actually bring relief down the road. Although I don't know if I've experienced significant relief up to this point, but I'm hoping that as I share my story and continue to deal with those deep feelings that I have held in for so long, that relief will begin to come. All I know is that I longed for serenity. I was holding out hope for another miracle. Beyond survival, I was now hoping for *peace.* Maybe at some point I would be able to move on with life...and love.

I was once at a Red Cross meeting and there were probably about twenty-five to thirty of us sitting in a circle with three of four therapists strategically placed among us. Most of us knew each other; we had been in the group for quite some time and were familiar with each other's issues and concerns.

One night a new fellow came in and joined the group and he was sitting on the other side of the circle from me. He started to talk, telling us his name and the role that he played at the World Trade Center site. He commenced to say that the fire and police departments didn't do anything at the site; that he was a one-man show, a hero. He was saying that the police and firefighters were drinking beer and all kinds of nonsense. As he chattered on, I became increasingly angry because of what he was saying. He kept talking about all the heroic acts that he performed. From his account, the first responders were useless while he practically performed miracles. So I became angry and said to myself, "When it's my turn, I am going to put him in his place..."

As a matter of fact, I noticed that as he was talking, some of the therapists and members who knew I was a former Fire Lieutenant would look at me to gauge my reaction. I had every intention of blasting him when it was my turn to talk. However, there were several other people who talked about their experiences of the collapse prior to me getting my turn. It was then that I had a change of heart. I thought about the guy who had said such outrageous things, realizing that he probably needed to express himself in that way because maybe he didn't know any better. Maybe that was his way of dealing with it, and who was I to judge that? So I just let it go. I turned the other cheek. I was trying to make the most of these sessions, even when they seemed to bring out the worse in me.

When it was my turn, I told the group that my name was Clarence Singleton and added that I was a retired New York City Fire Lieutenant. I glanced at the guy who had been so outspoken earlier, and saw his head drop quickly. I had a suspicion that he was kind of sorry about what he had said. And even if he wasn't, I felt better for showing restraint and self-control. After all, there was no way he could have known I was a Fire Lieutenant because I was sitting there in civilian clothes. However, that was the last time we saw him. He came to the meeting that one time and never returned.

Now I try hard every day to refrain from criticizing people for their behavior, and if I do, what I'm saying in fact is that I know better than God because I think everyone is exactly where God wants them to be at that particular time in their life: they have lessons to learn also. Ultimately, my trust is in God, and I know that when God is ready, He will move me from this place to the next place He has in store for me.

Chapter Nine - The Unexplained

I'm in love with the potential of **miracles**.
For me, the safest place is out on a limb.
~*Shirley MacLaine*

Clarence and his sister Ruby at the Pentagon in 2010.

One night at group therapy, I got the strength to share my story about being injured at the World Trade Center... the events that took place as my body was thrust to the ground, the challenge of getting up and coming to one wall that was too tall, and then finally about scaling the second wall. I described everything as best I could remember. It was very cathartic and it felt good to share after hearing the other stories.

But after I shared my story, a woman looked at me and said, "Clarence, I have worked down there for fifteen years, and there is no wall down there like the one you described."

I looked at her in amazement because I had gone back down to the scene several times looking for this wall, and I was never able to find it. As a matter of fact, one of my sons was with me down at the site one time when I was looking for the wall. He finally said, "Come on, Dad, give it up. You're not going to find that wall."

I couldn't explain it, but it was so real to me. The memory is one that I had replayed over and over in my head. Had I clung to it so long that it became real? Did I really climb that wall? Then I started to think about the fire marshal who I had met who didn't have any dust on him. I had never really stopped to think about why. I got a chill when I did.

I reminisced that after I had moved away from the area where I had seen the fire marshal, the EMS guys were the ones who helped me. I began to wonder, "Why didn't the fire marshal help me?" I didn't ask for his help, but as firefighters, we have a rule that we don't pass each other by if one needs help. He knew I was hurt. I also remember wondering at the time why the fire marshal didn't have any dust on him. Was my mind playing tricks on me or was it real? Or was it my way of coping?

When I shared this story in one of my group sessions, the therapists suggested strongly that I had just seen an apparition. I have prayed about it and thought long and hard about it. I am now quite sure of what I saw, and maybe it was an angel of the Lord for a number of reasons. I tried to think about it rationally, which of course is probably not the way we think about angels, but I had to process those events. I had to sift them through my memory to find out what really did happen.

First, the image I saw didn't have any dust on him, and that would have been impossible in the natural world in those horrific circumstances. Also, in the area down there I could not have seen a doorway with bright light coming through it because the buildings in the vicinity of the World Trade Center were massive; most cover the entire block and the sidewalks beside the buildings were very small. All the buildings were also locked, so it's not possible for me to have seen a doorway with light shining through it and for me to have seen the fire marshal standing there with no dust on him. Also, remember when I recounted that the EMS workers had to shine flashlights just to read signs, despite it being morning? Darkness was all around us. Light could not have happened naturally.

No, this was God, the all-powerful. A power that surpasses our understanding.

I remember that the fire marshal's first words to me when he saw me were, "I see you made it." That was kind of an affirmation telling me that I was alive. And he was right. I had made it. I just didn't realize that it would take much more time to make sense of it all.

From the time that I saw the image of the fire marshal standing in the doorway with bright light shining through the doorway until I saw the EMS guys who actually helped me to the ambulance, there was a period in there that I was wearing my glasses. It was only when I looked over the top of my glasses that I was able to see the EMS workers. Thinking back on that whole situation, I realize that there was so much dust stuck to my glasses that it would have been *impossible* for me to see the fire marshal through my glasses. My lenses were completely coated with dust after the collapse. After considering these factors, there is no doubt in my mind that the image dressed as a fire marshal was really an angel of the Lord.

I was saved for a reason.

You might think that this would be comforting. However, even with the realization that God has sent an angel to encourage me in the moments following the collapse, I still struggled with depression and survivor's guilt. Why was I saved and so many other moms and dads not? Why me and not the fire marshal himself? Why me and not the men I lost in Vietnam?

As the days blended together, I continued to work, but I found that I was depressed most of the time on my fire safety director's job. The level of depression was horrible and I still had a lot of pain in my shoulder from the dislocation. Looking back, I probably should not have gone to work, but should have taken time out to take care of myself. Yet, I was determined to try to get back to some type of normal. A new normal.

These were very fearful times in New York City in the days and weeks following the collapse of the Twin Towers. The impact of what had happened affected people in different ways. One of the most evident ways was reflected in how people of all ages responded to certain kinds of sounds—especially in Manhattan. I observed one distinct example of this kind of behavior at the building where I was working as a fire safety director.

During the course of a regular workday we had an alarm sound, which required all of the building workers to go outside until the all-clear signal was given. After the alarm stopped ringing and the test was over, I was using a megaphone-type bullhorn to inform the workers that it was safe for them to go back inside. However, none of them wanted to go back in the building; they were afraid to go back in because of what had happened on 9/11. There was nothing I could say to get them to go back inside. I told them that I was a retired Fire Lieutenant, reassuring them that we had checked the building out thoroughly, and there was no problem. Because of fear and the vivid memories of 9/11, they stayed outside for some time.

Eventually everyone went back in and resumed their duties, but any little noise that was heard in the building would trigger a fearful response, and the people would just run out into the streets. The devastation in New York City was catastrophic. Everywhere people looked, there were reminders of what had happened on 9/11. The smell of ash and death lingered in the air for weeks and weeks. Those vivid reminders prompted levels of fear greater than most people had ever experienced before and understandably so.

I faced similar challenges on many fronts. Anything and everything had the potential to remind me of the events of 9/11, and it all added to the depression I was experiencing on a daily basis. For example, because of the pain in my right shoulder, something as simple as shaking the hand of my boss even proved to be a painful, ongoing reminder of that fateful day at the World Trade Center.

Even now—over ten years after the collapse—I still struggle with the events of that fateful day. There are some occasions when certain things that transpire in a normal day become reminders of what happened at the World Trade Center on September 11. A frequent example of this happens when I look at a digital clock, and the time is 9:11. Whether it's 9:11 in the morning or at night, I always think of the collapse. I don't know why, but for whatever reason it just seems that whenever I look at the clock, morning or evening, it's 9:11. Every time it happens, I think, "Why couldn't I have looked at the clock when it was 9:10 or 9:12." I don't understand it, but it just seems like most of the time my digital clock says 9:11 when I look at it. In my head, I know it's *just a clock*, but when it displays "9:11," the enormity of what those numbers represent— the pain, the loss, the devastation, the fear and uncertainty—it all comes thundering back as the images of that day return in some form to haunt me again.

Chapter Ten – Acknowledging the Feelings

Cherish your emotions and never undervalue them.
~Robert Henri

Clarence carries injured woman in Vietnam.

Emotions are so hard to understand, so complicated. There's no doubt in my mind that I learned to suppress my feelings early on in Vietnam while I was in the Marine Corps. I have recognized this tendency to avoid dealing with my feelings on several occasions through the years.

For example, I remember one time before 9/11, when I was a firefighter, we had to run down to Greenwich Village in response to an emergency, and I was driving the fire truck south on 7th Avenue. Just as we came by St. Vincent's Hospital in lower Manhattan, I needed to make a right turn on 11th Street. My light was green, but I could hear the air horns from another fire truck blowing. I recognized my friend, from a neighboring ladder company, who was driving the other fire truck. We had worked together for several years, so we recognized each other's techniques, even behind the wheel.

On this day protocol dictated that my truck had priority, which meant that all other companies let you go first. However, instinct told me that my friend was not going to stop, even though I had a green light and his light was red. For whatever reason, I applied the brakes and as soon as I did, he blew right past me! If I had inched out into the intersection at all, there would have been a terrible accident.

When we got to the site of the emergency, after everything was over, he came to me and apologized. We said a few more words to each another before heading back to our respective firehouses, but I remember, even though I had come so close to death—or at least a horrible accident—that I had shrugged it off. After all, tough Marines don't talk about feelings, do they?

I still feel sad at times when thoughts come to me about the World Trade Center. It's difficult for me to think about the last moments of my friends and coworkers as the Towers collapsed and the debris covered them like a massive avalanche. In many cases the bodies of some of the guys were never found...no helmets or turnout coats...they were just turned to dust, along with the desks and furnishings of the offices and businesses. These brave first responders, many of whom were my friends and coworkers, are gone but not forgotten.

Several days after 9/11, I was down in the area where the World Trade Center had once stood. As I walked past Trinity Church I noticed some photos of many of the 9/11 victims that were posted on the fence outside the church. As I paused to look at them, I was shocked to see a picture of my friend—the one whom I had almost crashed into (or vice versa). As soon as my eyes fell on his photo, I immediately thought, "Oh no! He was killed also!" I was stunned because I had not known that he was one of the 343 firefighters who perished in the collapse.

A sense of sadness swept over me as I thought about my friend because he was a great guy, and we had been a good team in the fire department when we were responding to alarms. We had survived one near-miss years before, and what was the sense of it all? We survived that incident only to have him die on that tragic day.

I picked up my pace as I hurried past the remaining photos of victims displayed on the fence at Trinity Church. My heart was sad, and I didn't want to discover other familiar faces among the pictures hanging on the fence.

Right after the collapse on September 11, I attended a memorial for one of the firefighters that was killed from my former firehouse, Ladder 12. Out of respect I was wearing my lieutenant's dress blue uniform. One of the lieutenants that I worked under before I was promoted was also present for the memorial service. He had worked long hours at the site and had made it known that although the fire department was paying overtime wages to work down at the site, he did not want to take pay to help with the rescue efforts. When he saw me, he used me as an example, saying, "Look at guys like Clarence. They're retired and they came in to help out without any pay."

Included in the nearly 3,000 people who perished on September 11 in the World Trade Center collapse are 343 of our comrades from the fire department. (This number—343—equals almost half the number of on-duty deaths in the department's 100-year history.) The highest ranking member of the fire department that was killed on 9/11 was the Chief of the Department, Chief Peter Ganci, Jr. He was a very nice guy, and one of those 343 brave firefighters who lost their lives on September 11, 2001. The senseless loss of so many lives in one day was very difficult for me to accept.

If it had been possible, I would have attended *every* funeral or memorial service to honor the memory of the first responders who died that day. However, there were an overwhelming number of funerals and memorial services held around that time. I could only make one of the actual funerals, and one memorial service because it was emotionally overwhelming and too much for me to bear. We had a memorial at our firehouse for a few of the firefighters that perished. After being at the site and seeing all the destruction on 9/11, attending a funeral or memorial brought back so many difficult memories. The mental images of what happened at the site played over and over in my mind and were too painful to deal with. While I have struggled with depression and the emotional trauma of 9/11 and still face challenges at times, my personal faith and trust in God has helped me where nothing else could. I'm certain that God has brought me through all that I've been through to pass a message of hope on to others.

It's hard to comprehend that much loss, though. According to Wikipedia and other resources, the following statistics represent some of the key statistics related to 9/11:

- More than 90 countries lost citizens in the attacks on the World Trade Center on September 11, 2001, totaling 353 foreign nationals in all.

- Only 14 people escaped from the impact zone of the South Tower after it was hit and only four people from the floors above it. Individuals escaped from as high up on the South Tower as the 91st floor after the initial impact. They are reported to have escaped by means of Stairwell A, the only stairwell which had been left intact after the impact. It is speculated that this stairwell in the South Tower remained passable until the South Tower collapsed at 9:59 a.m. After the collapse of the Towers, only 23 survivors who were in or below the Towers escaped from the debris, including 15 rescue workers.

- Before the Twin Towers collapsed, it is estimated that 200 people jumped to their deaths from the burning

Towers, landing on the streets and rooftops of adjacent buildings hundreds of feet below. To witnesses who were watching, a few of the people who fell from the Towers seemed to have tumbled or jumped out of broken windows.

- Two thousand children lost a parent on September 11, including 146 who lost a parent at the Pentagon.

- A total of 1,337 vehicles were crushed when the Towers collapsed, including 91 FDNY vehicles.

The last survivor to be removed alive from the World Trade Center collapse debris was a Port Authority employee named Genelle Guzman-McMillan, who was removed at 12:30 p.m. on September 12—27 hours after the initial collapse. She worked on the 64th floor of the North Tower. She shared later that when the building collapsed around her she was not a person of faith at that time, but began to ask God to do a miracle for her. During the 27-hour ordeal, she said a man named Paul found her and promised to stay with her and hold her hand until she was rescued. When she was finally found in the rubble of the collapse, she was asleep and standing in an upright position. After she was successfully rescued, she asked her rescuers where Paul was so she could personally thank him for staying with her and holding her hand through the long and frightening ordeal. She was informed that there was no fireman named Paul with them and no one was seen with her when she was rescued. Freed at last from the rubble she knew that her prayers had been answered, and God had performed the miracle she had prayed for. I guess I was not the only person saved by an angel that day.

I have a copy of the *New York Times* that honored the 343 firefighters that perished at the site on 9/11. On very few occasions have I looked at all of the faces. I don't think I've ever counted how many friends I lost that day. I was recently asked if I knew how many of my friends and coworkers perished at the site, but I didn't have the answer. I just don't have what it takes to go look at each name or face. I'm sure it's many more than I realize or could imagine. I work at acknowledging the feelings that I know I have avoided at times. I know it's part of the healing. But the magnitude of that much loss is too great, so I take baby steps at times.

Every day, when I least expect it, the image of some of their faces come to mind. For example, Michael Judge was the fire department's Chaplain. We were good friends. We would see each other at fires. He would show up and we would tease each other and joke around a little bit. He was not the first one that was killed at the site, but he got the first death certificate. He is honored in the same *Life Magazine* where my photo appeared in the centerfold section of the publication. As I recall, Chaplain Michael is honored on the page before the photo of me on the hospital gurney. In the photo, three firefighters are shown carrying his body out of the rubble of the collapse. He was a man who dedicated himself to both God and his faith—and the fire department.

One day as I was looking for a meditation book to read, I came across a book that Father Michael had given to me. When I first picked up the book, though, I didn't realize that it was a book that was given to me by him. However, when I opened it, a little card fell out that had been tucked inside the cover. It was one of his fire department Chaplain cards. I picked it up and seeing his card made me feel a pang in my heart, made me feel sad again. Inside the front cover was an inscription that he had written to me. The short inscription read: "Clarence, some great thoughts for a great man in a great program for a greater life. Love Michael Judge." It was as if he had given me this book some fifteen years earlier to pass a message on to me. I read daily quotes from it, and think of him each time I pick up the book. Although my friend Michael Judge is gone, he's not forgotten. And even from heaven, his thoughtfulness reaches out to me and helps me when I am praying and meditating.

I wonder about one other little miracle. A few years before the World Trade Center collapse on 9/11, I was trying to get my sons to follow in my footsteps and join the fire department. My oldest son went all the way to the investigation portion. He took the written test and passed that with flying colors. He did well in every area, even though he was in college at the same time down in North Carolina. His schedule didn't allow for much extra time for studying for the fire department exam, yet when he went in and took the test, he almost aced it perfectly. He came up to take the physical portion, and aced that as well. Later the fire department called him in for the investigation part of the hiring process, and he decided not take the job.

I have often wondered if he had taken the job, where would he have been on September 11?

For that reason, I don't really push my children to go into any direction. I tell them what I think, and it's their choice whether or not they want to pursue that career. My son finished his study program and graduated from college. He has a good job now as a chemist. He decided to stay down in North Carolina, and that's where he is to this day. Looking back on that day and all the tragic scenes my eyes beheld, I'm grateful he wasn't there.

Chapter Eleven - Vietnam and 9/11

No event in American history is more misunderstood than
the Vietnam War. It was misreported then,
and it is misremembered now.
~Richard Nixon

Clarence fills sandbags in Vietnam.

In Vietnam in 1968 I was with the second battalion, 9th
Marines. This was a very tough unit. Most of us came back to
the States either wounded or in a casket. So much has been
written about the Vietnam War and the horrific things that took
place there. Yet, my time in Vietnam doesn't even compare to what
I saw on September 11, 2001. I had not known the magnitude of
destruction and the loss of lives in one day of being in Vietnam like
I did at the World Trade Center on that fateful day. The experience

was very frightening because I had never seen or been involved in anything as large and destructive as the collapse.

While I was at Ground Zero on 9/11 my mind would not allow me to comprehend the enormity and the full extent of what had happened. When I first arrived, the South Tower was already down...something once deemed impossible. The second Tower was still standing, but it was burning and smoking profusely. There was a feeling of such vulnerability, and I just couldn't imagine being attacked at home. It was inconceivable, and I felt total despair and refused to believe what I was seeing. This once-familiar landscape was now strewn with debris and twisted metal, and the vastness of the scene seemed to melt into the horizon. Later that night, while watching the tragedy play over and over on the television news, the depths of the collapse consumed me. My self-defense mechanisms, which I had subconsciously learned to use in Vietnam and in the fire department to protect me from emotionally disturbing events, were overloaded and nothing was in place to absorb the shock of the collapse. The tragedy of 9/11 was the straw that broke the camel's back as far as my emotions are concerned.

In Vietnam, I experienced a lot of trauma over the course of days, weeks, and months. At the collapse on 9/11, it was one unbelievable tragedy that took place in a matter of a few hours. There aren't words to describe all that my eyes beheld that day. There are still moments when some of those images seem more like scenes from a movie than reality.

I have thought about it repeatedly, and I have come to the conclusion that the events of 9/11 had a much greater and more traumatic impact on me than my eleven months and fourteen days of service in Vietnam. Ultimately, there is really no accurate comparison to make between Vietnam and the World Trade Center collapse because when the battle is brought home to your own backyard, it's personal and you feel it more. Being in Vietnam, I was doing my duty; I was far from home and I was there to do a job. In Vietnam I saw so much destruction and devastation, but it still didn't have the same effect on me that the World Trade Center did because this new battle was being fought at home. It was brought to my doorstep, and it was an attack against me, along with all the other citizens of our great nation.

In a strange twist, now I can understand how the Vietnamese people felt about having a war fought in their country. It's a really devastating, horrible thing...one that can take years to recover from. It is a trauma striking places that are familiar to you. After 9/11, we New Yorkers would stare into the gaping wound in the earth and think of what was once there.

One thing, however, that has gotten me through both Vietnam and 9/11 is a childhood "hero" of sorts. When I was young, there was a comic about a soldier named "Sergeant Rock." Sgt. Frank Rock was introduced by DC Comics in 1959. What struck me then was a slogan of his about how "together we move forward." You see, whether in Vietnam, as part of my ladder company, or on 9/11, there was always a sense of either my platoon or my fire station sticking together. Maybe that was another reason 9/11 pained us so much. So many people perished at once, and despite first responders racing to the site, despite doctors and nurses racing to hospitals to do what they could, the Red Cross coming down to Ground Zero, all of it, could not save all those souls.

But for me, compounding the events of Vietnam with 9/11 meant I developed post-traumatic stress disorder. It was insidious, the way the changes occurred in me.

I've always been active, working most of my life. During my tenure in the fire department, I was also working a second job as a mortgage inspector on a part-time basis for fifteen years; I was always on the go. I realized later through a veteran's group that I was actually a workaholic because I was suppressing all of the feelings that I carried from Vietnam. If I kept busy enough, I didn't think about things.

After 9/11, I began to notice times of memory lapse and memory loss. I would call friends that I had spoken with the day before, with no recollection of our previous conversation. When I asked my doctor about it, he said I shouldn't worry about it because I was getting older. (I was only about fifty-one years of age at the time.)

I finally addressed it and inquired about the topic at one of my group sessions, asking, "Can trauma cause memory loss?" The counselors and several people who were attending the group responded simultaneously with, "Yes, absolutely." Since then I have talked to several people who have also dealt with memory loss following a trauma and observed many similarities.

After the events at the World Trade Center site, my friend MaryAnn recognized that I had changed, but she didn't know what to do about it. She also sensed that I was suffering and felt powerless.

On more than one occasion she accompanied me in attending a group at the VA Hospital for therapy. There were a lot of veterans at each meeting, and often they came with their spouse or a good friend. In each meeting we would sit around and talk about our issues.

MaryAnn would usually go with me to try to learn what she could do to help my situation. I didn't realize it at the time, but she told someone that all I did was sit and stare at the walls in my house. It was true, but I didn't realize it until she said it. I could spend hours just sitting and staring. I couldn't tell you what was on my mind at the time, or what I was thinking about. It was like a dead spot with no memory. It was very scary.

My memory loss issues seemed to get worse as time marched on. Now I wasn't just losing time; I began to misplace various items on a regular basis. I eventually came to understand that this was due primarily to the trauma related to my experiences from Vietnam and the added trauma from 9/11. For example, if I put something down in the house arbitrarily, I forget where I put it. However, if I focused on the action, like putting my watch on the table, it was much more likely that I would recall where I had placed the item. To this day I have problems with my recall.

There was one time when I was planning on taking a trip to

South Carolina. I left the house and had to come back four different times to get things that I had forgotten. Now I try to lay everything out the night before so I can check to make sure everything is in my bag. Even then, I sometimes miss something or forget to take certain things that I will need.

Now I try to look on the bright side of things and one positive benefit that comes from my short-term memory problem is that I can watch a movie, and a couple weeks later I can watch the same movie again because I don't remember all the scenes from the first time that I watched it. So if my wife wants to watch the latest blockbuster again, that's just fine with me. Learning to recognize the bright spots in life has helped me tremendously! Remember, you just want to hold on to hope.

Chapter Twelve - Priceless Rewards

If you are going through hell, keep going.
~Winston Churchill

Clarence reunites with rescued victims Geralyn Hearne and her daughter Merry from the World Trade Center bombing in 1993.

Before 9/11, I had what seemed like a lifetime of fires and rescues. One of my most memorable events as a firefighter was when I rescued Geralyn Hearne when the World Trade Center was bombed the first time in 1993. I assisted in rescuing many other individuals that day as well, but Geralyn's story is extraordinary. Before I tell you what was so special about Geralyn's rescue, let me tell you how the day started out.

Every day is unique in the life of a firefighter. You never know what's going to happen or when an alarm will come in, so while you wait, you spend time at the firehouse. As you may know, this sometimes involves maintenance of the equipment or washing the trucks. At some point during the day, you will find the firefighters gathered in the kitchen and joking with one another.

I usually ate with the guys at the firehouse. It was standard daily practice for the company to go out, purchase the food, and divide the cost of the meal. Whatever the cost of the food that day, we would divide it by the number of guys who ate, and each firefighter would pay their portion.

On February 26, 1993, I didn't eat with the guys as usual. That morning we were near a Spanish restaurant so I went in and ordered some Spanish food and took it back to the firehouse for lunch. When we returned, the guys were in the process of preparing their meals, but I started eating right away.

I had just enjoyed my last fork full of food when the alarm came in for a fire at the World Trade Center. I got up from the table, and started putting on my gear. As I got ready I teased the guys, stating that I hoped the fire is in the basement, because after all that Spanish food, I was too heavy to walk up any stairs. We all laughed because I had really eaten a considerable amount of Spanish beans and rice with smothered chicken. As we joked and laughed, we had no idea the kind of horror awaited our arrival.

As we were getting ready back at the firehouse, we were unaware that at 12:17 p.m. a loud boom had rocked lower Manhattan when a massive explosion happened in the parking garage beneath the World Trade Center. As I was driving into the scene, the closer we got to the Twin Towers, the more traffic we encountered. Traffic usually accumulates in a fire area because of all the fire trucks coming into the vicinity and the curious people coming to see what's going on.

I was among the first responders. As we pulled up to the scene at the World Trade Center, we saw black smoke coming from the lower level. In my mind I assumed it was a transformer fire because it was coming from the basement area, and it was dense black smoke. As firefighters we have a way of telling what's burning by the color of the smoke.

As soon as we got to the area, we parked the truck and all of us went over to the chief to get our assignment. The chief is usually standing outside the fire building waiting for the trucks to come in. He is the one who tells you what area of the building he wants you to search.

Meanwhile, in the parking garage under the World Trade Center the explosion had carved out a huge crater several stories deep and several stories high. Smoke and flames from the explosives began filling the parking garage as well as streaming upward into the building. Some individuals were trapped in the offices, and on the street level others who were covered with soot and appeared to be panic-stricken were running out of the building. As the events unfolded that day, we learned that six people were killed almost instantaneously when the explosion happened, and in the end, more than 1,000 people were hurt, many with crushed limbs and various other injuries.

Since this was a high-rise building, each truck company was assigned five floors to search. Our company—12 Truck—was assigned to the 54th to the 58th floors. The elevators were out so we went into the building and found the staircase. As soon as we started our climb to the 54th floor, all of us shifted into rescue mode and left the laughing and joking for another time. We had work to do.

Darkness greeted us as we entered the stairway, because there was no electricity in the building. The only visible glow was the lights that we had strapped to our helmets as well as the handheld flashlight that each officer carries.

As we were heading up, we took the inside of the staircase. It was a little shorter. There was a constant stream of civilians coming down, and they took the outside of the staircase, which helped the flow of traffic on the stairs. As we were coming up all you could see were their legs walking down. There was of course a lot of commotion and chatter as they watched us ascend. "Wow, you guys are going up," and some of them were thanking us. Even at a time like that it was very nice to hear them say that because it kind of helps to get you motivated to continue your climb.

We had our full firefighting gear with us. That includes firefighter boots, turnout coats, helmets, a mask on our backs, and our tools. As always with the weight of all that equipment, it was a very difficult climb, especially to such high floors.

There was one firefighter from Brooklyn with us who was wearing bunker gear. When new equipment is given to the fire department, they disperse it to one unit at a time. Brooklyn had been given their bunker gear, but we were still wearing the individual pieces. The firefighter from Brooklyn was a young fellow, but he was struggling a little because the bunker gear was cumbersome and hot. However, when we got to the upper floors and he shed his gear, we couldn't keep up with him. He was like a rabbit and was running circles around us.

As we got to the 44th floor during our climb, some civilians came into the stairway and told us there was a lady on the floor having some medical problems. We went in and found her lying down with another woman nearby who was trying to help her. There was smoke in the stairway by this time, and a haze of smoke throughout the building. We looked at the woman on the floor, and she seemed to be doing okay. Because I had a handie-talkie radio, the officer said, "Clarence, you stay here with them and we're going to continue going up to the 54th floor." At the time we had 14 more floors to climb.

I acknowledged the officer's orders and the firemen continued on their way up the stairs to the 54th floor. So I'm there with these two women. One is lying on the floor and her friend is holding her hand. I didn't find out their names immediately, but I eventually learned that the name of the distressed woman on the floor was Geralyn, and her longtime friend, Donna, was there beside her, holding her hand. I also noticed that Geralyn was pregnant.

As I stood there watching Geralyn lying on the floor, she started convulsing. I looked at Donna and it was obvious that she was about to cry. With Geralyn still convulsing on the floor in front of us, I asked Donna if this had happened before. Donna replied, "No," as she continued to hold Geralyn's hand.

I got on my handie-talkie immediately to ask my officer and the other firefighters who had already left to go up to the 54th floor to come back to help, but I couldn't reach them. The frequency of our radios wasn't made to go great distances because if you're operating at a fire and there are other companies who are also operating at a fire in a nearby location, you could have radio interference. Since I was unable to contact them, I reached for the telephone on the desk to place a call on a land line. My intention was to call the dispatcher, and have the dispatcher notify the sector chief that the young lady my officer left me with was having some serious medical problems.

I decided to try my handie-talkie again. This time I made contact with my company, and they started back down toward the 44th floor. In the meantime, since there was a lot of smoke in the area, I took my mask off and applied it to Geralyn's face to help her breathe.

When my company came back to the area where we were, we decided to take Geralyn down to the 34th floor where there was a triage unit set up for injured people. We decided to transport her in a chair, which is common for firefighters. The victim is placed in the chair and four firefighters lift the chair—two in front and two in the back, each holding a leg of the chair as they lift the victim and carry the person to safety. Donna followed along behind.

As we were going down the stairs I was in front, responsible for carrying one of the front legs of the chair. The chair was scraping the stairs a little bit so we adjusted the position of the chair and kept moving down the stairway, intent on getting some help for Geralyn.

After we took Geralyn down to the 34th floor, there were some medical personnel there attending to several people. We stayed with her and Donna a little while before heading back up to our assignment on floor 54.

After climbing several flights of stairs, we heard over the radio that Geralyn's condition had worsened, so we ran back down to the triage unit. We stood around there and watched the EMS guys work on her to stabilize her condition. When it appeared that Geralyn's condition had stabilized, we headed back up to the 54th floor again.

I don't know how many minutes passed, but as we were climbing back up the stairs, we heard over the handie-talkie that Geralyn's condition had worsened again so we headed back down. This happened about three times. Even though the medical personnel were there and qualified to provide the emergency medical attention she needed, by this time we felt as if she was our patient. We knew she was in good hands, but we went back just in case she needed to be carried to the exterior of the building.

Eventually, we didn't hear any more talk about Geralyn's condition worsening over the handie-talkie. However, there was a lot of radio talk about her that day that went on for a few hours. By hearing bits and pieces of the communications, I could tell that she was still in the building and still on the 34th floor.

After a while, there was no talk about Geralyn coming over the radio, and I said to myself, "Great," because that was an indication that she was out of the building and getting medical attention at the hospital.

My company and I were already doing our searches on the 54th floor, and working our way up to the 58th floor. At one point, I took a moment to use the land line to call my then-wife at work and let her know I was okay. Then I continued with the search, going in and out of the staircase on the floors with the other firefighters, searching for victims and people stranded in the building. As we moved from floor to floor, we would encounter workers in some of the offices; many of them were understandably afraid, but fortunately they were alive.

On one occasion, while we were searching one of the floors, I had to act very calm to maintain order. I took my helmet off to appear less intimidating and went over to the desk and put my feet up on the top of it. I was talking to the people, and I'd get up and walk over to the window to maintain that calm effect. As a rescuer you don't want to show a lot of excitement because you don't want to encourage a sense of panic in the civilians. We told the folks to head down the stairs toward the street, and we continued on our mission to search the building. On several floors there were people trapped in the elevators. When the power went out in the building because of the blast, all of the electricity was destroyed so if you were unfortunate enough to have been in an elevator, you were stuck there. So, as is common with a tragedy of that size and with such a huge building, we ended up performing a lot of elevator rescues that day.

At one point, one of the workers from the building came over and told us a fellow employee was missing. He said the missing person was one of the building workers and he had a handie-talkie with him. He said, "The last I heard from him he was on the 64th floor stuck in an elevator, but he must be out because I haven't heard from him lately."

We said, "We can't go on hearsay. We have to see him, because anything could have happened." The battery life of those little radios doesn't last indefinitely. You have to recharge the batteries periodically, so we thought the battery could have died or something could be wrong with him so we couldn't go on an assumption that he was "probably fine."

We started looking for this guy who was supposedly trapped in an elevator; although we thought they were all cleared, it's always possible that we missed one. We started on the 55th floor, checking elevators and tapping on the walls where the elevator shafts run through. We had to be very thorough because some of them were blind shafts, which meant that an elevator would take you from the 1st floor to 40th floor. Some call them express elevators because between those two steps there are no access points or landings. With that in mind, we kept tapping on the walls, hoping to find the missing worker.

We finally got to the 65th floor, and we were in a large office. I tapped on the wall, and I got a tap back. Inside I was like "Yeah!" so I told the lieutenant, "I've got him!"

We tapped again and the person in the elevator tapped back. Next we breached a hole in the wall in the office, and when we looked down, it was a shaft all the way down to the 1st floor. We scratched our heads and asked, "What is going on here? Where did the tapping sound come from?"

We still couldn't see the elevator, so I came up with an idea. Since there was a large floor area, I left the little room where we breached the wall. I paced down about twenty feet to an interior office hallway and walked over to the other side of the office, which is about fifteen feet over. Then I paced twenty feet back where I found myself standing in front of a restroom. I pointed at the rear wall of the restroom and told the boss, "He's over here!"

Through a process of deduction it dawned on me that it could be a blind shaft and the elevator could run behind the bathroom. With that in mind, I went into the bathroom and tapped on the wall and someone inside the elevator tapped back. They were just on the other side of that wall.

We breached the wall and forced the elevator door open, and there was the worker from the building that we were looking for, along with a few other civilians. We got him out, and by this time we had teamed up with a company from Brooklyn, Ladder 156. We were working together, and did additional searches of the area. In the end we each had dust all over us from breaching the elevators.

One thing about being in the fire department is we like our helmets to look "salty," which is a term that means a little scorched from the heat of the fires we had been in. We like that old burnt look. At this time, Brooklyn wasn't issued new helmets yet, but in Manhattan they were, and I was one of the guys wearing a brand-new helmet with a piece of paper on the helmet with my company's number on it. I was thinking, "Man, these guys coming from Brooklyn with their salty helmets, and I look like a guy who just started as a probationary firefighter." On some occasions I had to tell them that I had been on the job for many years. I took some pictures, and after I had them developed, I took them over to Ladder 156 in Brooklyn and gave them to the guys to keep.

With 12 Truck's fire-floor search complete, the chief told us to begin the arduous climb down. During the course of this day, we climbed well over 100 flights of stairs. There was no way of stopping me. I have that Marine Corps attitude. I am going to complete the mission, no matter what.

Now it was time to walk down all those steps we had climbed as we searched for victims. While we were walking back down, it seemed like we were never going to reach the 1st floor so we could exit out into the street. After climbing so many flights of stairs, the descent is difficult and your legs ache because you use different muscles in your legs climbing down than you did when you were climbing up the stairs.

When we finally reached the 1st floor and got out into the street, we learned that it wasn't a transformer fire as we had suspected. Details were just being released about a bomb that was placed in the basement of the building that had been detonated. Nothing like this had ever happened before within the borders of our nation, and no one realized the ramifications of what had happened that day.

We got back on the fire truck and started to head back to the firehouse. I was the chauffeur so I was the one doing the driving. I was exhausted from walking up all those stairs, from forcing elevators open and breaching walls all day. Then there was Geralyn...I wondered how she was doing. It had been a long day. I wasn't in good shape mentally either, so I took my time as I drove back to the firehouse.

We got back to the station, and I was still thinking about Geralyn. I wondered how she was doing; I was worried about her. I got off duty and took a shower before leaving the firehouse. Next, I drove back to Brooklyn and was still deeply concerned about Geralyn's outcome. She had looked so helpless and then there was the pregnancy to consider as well.

When morning came on February 27, I was so stiff and sore that I couldn't get out of bed; I couldn't even walk. In fact, I had to roll out of bed onto the floor and lay there for a while, working my body until it loosened up a bit. I was aching from the climb the day before, and I felt like every muscle was throbbing.

My wife (at that time) and I were watching TV while we got ready for the day. As I glanced at the news at one point, there was a picture of Geralyn on the screen with a report about her becoming sick and being rescued at the World Trade Center. Pointing toward the television, I shouted to my wife, "That's her!"

The news report went on to say that she and her premature baby were in St. Vincent's Hospital in Manhattan. My wife and I immediately got dressed and went over to visit her. When we arrived at the hospital, I told the receptionist who I was looking for and the reason why it was so important. I found out what room Geralyn was in, and my wife and I headed up to her room.

When we walked in, there were people sitting around talking and Geralyn was in the bed. Geralyn had a dumbfounded look on her face, as if to say, "Who are these people and what are they doing *here*?" You see, Geralyn and the others in the room are Caucasian and we are African American. So, clearly we weren't related! She probably assumed we entered the wrong room.

I didn't wait for any questions. I introduced myself and told her that I was one of the firefighters who rescued her. In a moment everyone's face lit up. Geralyn's mother was there, and she gave me one of the biggest hugs. That made me feel so good. Such extraordinary circumstances had brought our lives together. We exchanged phone numbers that day, and in the months and years that followed we kept in touch and became very good friends.

St. Vincent's Hospital was just down the street from our firehouse, so I convinced the guys to take the truck down and go see Geralyn and the baby. The baby was named Meredith, but she was called "Merry" for short. We went in to see the baby and Merry was so small that she could easily fit in the palm of your hand with room to spare. When she was born she was so tiny, weighing only one pound and nine ounces. She was a little miracle born out of the rubble of terrorism, a reminder that hope and faith are always stronger than darkness.

A few days later there was going to be a news interview in the hospital lobby for Geralyn. I got a call from the fire department's

PR unit; they wanted to talk to me because I was going to be a part of the interview. They wanted to make sure that I was a good speaker since I was a representative of the fire department.

On the day of the interview my wife and I went down to the hospital. I was wearing my "class A's"—the firefighter's dress uniform. There was a group of reporters from TV, radio and the newspapers sitting in the lobby. The director of the hospital came over to me at one point and said, "Wow, it was a great thing you did to rescue Geralyn."

I said, "You know, it was no big deal. I was just doing my job," which is what most rescuers say. "We were just doing our job..."

The hospital director looked at me and said, "Clarence, it is a big deal! You rescued this young lady. She was pregnant, and her body was expelling the baby. The mother and baby would have died if you guys weren't there to help. Because you were there, they are both alive."

Her words touched me deeply, and I realized she was right. God had given us the strength to actually save a life...Geralyn's life and her baby's life, too.

I changed my outlook on the way I thought about that situation. As a matter of fact, it changed my perspective on all of the other situations that were to come in the future when I rescued people... they are big deals! They should be celebrated!

We were sitting at some tables for the interview along with two EMS guys who were part of the rescue that took care of Geralyn. Donna, her friend, was there—still by her side—and Geralyn's mother. Geralyn was in a wheelchair because she still wasn't able to walk at this point, and then there was my wife and me, as well as some of the staff from the hospital.

We were sitting there, and I have to admit: I was nervous. The reporters talked to several of the rescuers and the doctors. During the interview the doctors explained that Geralyn had a condition called eclampsia. At one point I looked out into the audience where the reporters were, and I saw a reporter I recognized from one of the TV stations looking at me. My heart started pounding and I thought, "I'm next...he's going to call on me and ask me questions," which he did.

I answered his questions and explained how we had performed the job that the chief had given us, where and how we had found Geralyn, and how we got her down to the triage area. I was pleased with how the interview went.

Also at the interview was Mayor Dinkins; he was the mayor of New York at the time. Cardinal O'Connor was also there. When my wife saw Cardinal O'Connor, she gave him a hug and started laughing and said, "Oops! I don't know if I was supposed to hug you!" He just laughed.

During the interview, Donna was talking about what had happened and she called me by my first name as she spoke. One of the reporters said, "I see you've gotten to know these firefighters very well... you're calling them by their first name!" We all just laughed, never realizing at the time what a wonderful friendship would develop from our chance meeting on the 44th floor.

A few days later *The New York Newsday*, a daily newspaper serving Long Island and New York City, ran two articles about the rescue of Geralyn and Meredith during the bombing of the World Trade Center on February 26, 1993. One article, which was titled "1 lb. 9 oz. ... The Littlest Survivor" dealt briefly with the rescue of Geralyn and the birth of Meredith. The second covered more details about the complexity of a rescue under such difficult circumstances.

Each time I talk about rescuing Geralyn and her unborn child, it always brings a smile to my face. Words can't describe the feeling that comes with saving a life, and that day I was privileged to save both Geralyn and her baby. It was such a wonderful feeling. I have probably talked about this rescue thousands of times because it is the most meaningful to me of all the rescues I ever experienced.

When Merry arrived on February 26, 1993, she came into the world facing incredible odds of survival. Yet, she grew up to be so smart. Through the years I have kept in touch with Geralyn, Meredith, and Donna since we first met on February 26, 1993. I felt a sense of pride when I learned that Merry did so well in high school that she was taking college courses while attending high school and is considering a career in medicine.

Merry graduated from high school in 2011, and I was invited to a backyard celebration in her honor. I traveled from Virginia to Metuchen, New Jersey for the event. I wouldn't have missed it for the world. My friend, MaryAnn, went with me, and it was such a moving experience to be reunited with Geralyn, Merry, and Geralyn's friend, Donna. Words aren't adequate to describe what I felt as I watched Merry and all her friends celebrate her graduation and her amazing life. My heart was so full...it was like Christmas and the Fourth of July at the same time! It was such a joy to see these who hold such a special place in my heart again: Geralyn, Merry, and Donna.

I didn't know all the people that were there so Geralyn introduced me and told them that I had saved her life. During the celebration Meredith presented me with a cap and medallion of the *U.S.S. New Yorker,* the ship that was built from World Trade Center scrap metal. She gave me the cap first, and I gave her a hug and a kiss. She left and came back with the medallion, and I got another hug and a kiss. She chuckled when I told her to keep giving me gifts because I could keep getting kisses and hugs from her. As we spent time together that weekend, we laughed and shared so many special moments. Seeing them again and being with them brought back so many memories connected with that day the World Trade Center was bombed...but this time the memories were happy memories and the tears were tears of joy. Such special acts don't always come out of such tragedies, but I was just glad this turned out so well.

Geralyn didn't know it at the time, but a little later through newspaper articles she found out that I was a veteran from Vietnam, adding that her father was a veteran from World War II. Geralyn believed it was as if her father had sent me to help her. She also said that she couldn't have been in better hands. Another angel working in the Towers? Who knows?

Even though I can't explain it, I believe that there is a realm beyond the natural where miracles happen. There have been times when I've been in tough situations, and have thought of my mom first. I've often wondered why I didn't call on God then. Things have changed, though, and now it has been God first that I've called upon for help, and He has always come to my rescue.

The fire department ended up awarding me a medal for rescuing Geralyn. One day each year, the fire department has a ceremony for passing out medals for firefighters who have performed heroic acts during the previous year. However, in 2002, I received a very special award in a ceremony held at Rutgers University.

On April 17, 2002, Geralyn Hearne, and I were invited to Rutgers University in New Jersey to speak at a multi-cultural affair. The event we were to speak at was held a few months after 9/11.

There was a large student body present. I went wearing my lieutenant's dress blue uniform. Just prior to the time for me to speak, some footage was shown of the collapse of the World Trade Center. As the film began, I saw a firefighter up there on the screen that I had known for quite some time. He had been on the job for about thirty years. I saw him in the film after the first Tower had collapsed on 9/11. He had the look of despair on his face. I had never seen that look on his face before. He was always smiling. It made me remember our last meeting.

I was at his firehouse one day, Rescue 1 in Manhattan, prior to 9/11. We were sitting around in the kitchen talking and one of the conversations was about his helmet that fell into a previous fire and the chiefs were trying to get him to stop wearing it, but he refused. I recall joking with him that day about his charred up helmet. That was the last time that I remember talking to him.

At the World Trade Center site after the first Tower had collapsed, I suspected that he was looking for his son, because his son was on the job that day as well. He had a worried look on his face. Sadly, both he and his son lost their lives on September 11 at the collapse. I got choked up as tears came to my eyes. I was feeling very sad. I was hoping that I would be able to compose myself before I was called to the podium.

As I was introduced, the student body welcomed me with applause that seemed to go on and on. When the applause subsided, I shared my story about what had happened to me and what I had seen at the World Trade Center on September 11. Even though I had prepared my speech, talking about the events of 9/11 always evoked deep emotion in me. I was so nervous that the microphone was shaking in my hands, but I felt I did my best, and I was pleased with what I said to the students.

After I finished speaking, I was awarded The Unsung Hero Award. It was presented to me for both the rescue of Geralyn in 1993 and my actions during the collapse of the Twin Towers on September 11. It reads: "The State University of New Jersey, Rutgers College Educational Opportunity Program Student Association and the Hearne family presents Clarence Singleton The Unsung Hero Award on the 17th day of April, 2002. Brave, Bold, and Courageous, you were willing to risk your life so that others could live. We honor you for your heroism on February 26, 1993, and September 11, 2001, and every day of your life."

In addition to receiving The Unsung Hero Award that day, an article from *Home News Tribune* dated March 21, 2002, was attached to the plaque that chronicled what happened.

Whenever I read something about Geralyn's rescue, my eyes fill with tears...not tears of sadness, but tears of immeasurable joy. The article also mentioned I had put my life on the line to save others, and I guess that did happen. Amazingly, I had no concern for myself. Helping other people was all that mattered. I can't help it. I am just, I've decided, hard-wired to be a rescuer.

Looking back in retrospect, it was the right thing and a good thing to do. I just wish more people would reach out to others. I wish people would quit all the fighting and bickering and just enjoy life because no matter how many years we have to live; life is short in the grand scheme of things. It is more fruitful to help people rather than tear them down. I am grateful for I know it is God working through me to help these people, and I will continue to help people as long as I'm alive and as long as God gives me the strength to do so.

In fire department jargon I've always loved "being at the big ones," meaning big fires and emergencies. It just seemed to be part of my nature. I was talking to a friend about my time in Vietnam, the Marines and the fire department and he asked, "Why do you do these heroic things and put yourself in these dangerous situations?" Actually, the only time I can recall putting myself in dangerous situations is when someone needs my assistance, and it's a calculated risk. I'm risking my life to save theirs. Thus far, I've had some close calls and narrow escapes, but I'm still standing.

Chapter Thirteen — Segregation and Beyond

There never was a good war or a bad peace.
~Benjamin Franklin

Clarence secures the perimeter in Vietnam.

Everything was new to me in the military, and Vietnam was so different from Sumter, South Carolina, where I had grown up. Like many during that time, my family was poor and in the South, segregation was the norm. Blacks and whites ate in different restaurants, went to separate movie theaters, and drank from different water fountains. I was one of those African Americans you've probably heard about who rode in the back of the city buses until The Civil Rights Act became law. However, Vietnam was a different story.

Unlike my hometown, there were no racial barriers in Vietnam. It was a welcome change. We all treated one another with respect. The unity was wonderful. That's why it was shocking to see the separation again when we got back to the States. I had forgotten that people didn't speak to you if you were a different color. Some veterans were shunned when they returned to the States, and some were even called names like "baby killers."

In Vietnam our unit had bonded. We all would do anything to help out the next Marine. We stood shoulder to shoulder and fought as one unit, proudly serving our nation together.

All the Marines that I served with got along very well. I have heard some stories from other Marines that there were some problems with their platoon, but I never experienced anything like that in mine. Whenever we saw each other, we'd give each other high-five signs or victory signs or something like that. We'd share water from canteens, and we took care of each other. This training helped me years later when I was wearing a different uniform, that of a firefighter. Just like firefighters, when a Marine went down, everyone was there to help out in whatever way they could.

The Million-Dollar Stare

There was a guy that I had gone through boot camp with. He was a very big, tall, strong guy...very tough. He was in a convoy one day, and he passed the bridge that we were guarding. As he passed us he stopped, and I noticed that he was raggedy and he really smelled. He had a look on his face that we called the "million-dollar stare" — when you just stare at a person, and the eyes are almost piercing right through you.

I remember feeling sorry for him that day because he smelled so bad, but shortly after I was in the same situation. It didn't take long to discover that sometimes we wouldn't shower for weeks or months at a time. The only water we touched was when it rained or when we crossed streams. After a while everybody smelled horrible, and when everyone smells the same, you don't even notice the odor. I imagine if we were around someone who wasn't accustomed to the smell, it would really be something.

I never had much facial hair, and I still don't. In boot camp on Parris Island, after we would go into the bathroom for shaving and showering, once we were on our way out, the drill instructor would always stand by the door. If any of the Marines hadn't shaved perfectly, he would stand there with his cigarette lighter and actually burn the stubs off! It is a tough life being in the Marine Corps, so you wanted to make sure you followed orders to stay out of trouble.

There were many facets of training during boot camp. Some prepared us for physical tasks and others prepared us mentally. One of the aspects of training that I didn't care for during boot camp was the gas chamber. They put us in this gas chamber, which was completely sealed. At first we had our masks on. However, after being in there for a period of time we had to take the mask off and run around in the chamber reciting the Marine Corps Hymn. You couldn't get out of the gas chamber until they let you out so it was quite a painful experience. Your nose would run, and your eyes got red and burned so your goal was to stay nice and calm as you sang the Marine Corps Hymn. Once they opened the door, onlookers would see a stream of Marines running as fast as they could go because you had to run to get the stuff out of your system, out of your lungs, and off your clothes.

The gas had a horrible smell. Even though that training was very difficult, it worked and was for our own good. Later when I was in Vietnam, we got whiffs of gas from time to time, and right away everybody ran for the gas masks. Even though the training was a difficult experience, it was well worth it because it saved many lives in combat.

We also learned weapons care. A Marine relies on his weapon because it could mean the difference between living and dying on the battlefield. In the Marine Corps, we took a lot of pride in the care and maintenance of our rifles. Each Marine was responsible for his own weapon, including keeping his rifle clean and knowing every single part of it and how it functioned. We would drill with our rifles constantly. In fact, we got so good at it that part of our training included taking it apart blindfolded and putting it back together again. After performing this exercise several times, we were so skilled that we could take it apart and put it back together again just by feeling it. This kind of training prepares you for battle situations and potentially helps you in a war zone. Even if you don't have your sight, you still know your weapon, and you are able to assemble and reassemble it in battle. This, of course, would increase your chances of survival.

Part of our training also involved pugil stick fights for self-defense. It's not a familiar term to most, but every Marine knows what a pugil stick is. They have a soft padding on each end and looks something like an extended ax handle. We were simulating fighting with rifles with bayonets attached, learning with pugil sticks as we prepared for what we might face in battle.

On our first day of practicing with them, I was the first one from our platoon to try to use it. I volunteered to go out and fight another Marine using the device. We fought, and I got the best of him and beat him up with the pugil stick.

After it was over, all the Marines from our platoon were standing around and the drill instructor asked everyone who they thought had won. Everyone said, "Singleton did." The drill instructor responded, "Nope, the other guy did because he touched Clarence with the pugil stick first. If that had been an actual rifle with a bayonet attached, he would have been dead."

Without hesitating I said, "OK, give me another shot at him."

The drill instructor obliged. When the Marine charged at me with the pugil stick, I stepped aside and hit him a few times. He fell on the ground, and I continued to pound on him with the pugil stick. I finally threw it down and asked, "Who won now?"

There were many aspects to life as a Marine, and most of the time the conditions weren't easy to deal with. Sometimes we were short on food and the C-rations were scarce. There were nights when we were so cold after the temperatures dropped from the stifling, humid daytime heat we had endured before the sun went down. Bathing was often just a memory because we weren't able to wash up for weeks at a time. Consequently, the only water that touched us was the water that we waded through on patrol. Yet, through all of that I was never sick.

Back then we were tough young guys...most of us were just eighteen or nineteen years of age. Sometimes we'd walk through the tall bamboo grass and those razor-sharp leaves would cut us up real good! In fact, I still have scars from bamboo grass cuts on my hands and one on my stomach area. Sometimes when there was a lot of grass, if we were going to set up camp there, we would have to clear a field of fire so we could see in all directions around us. At first we stomped on the bamboo grass and pounded it down with our feet so we would have visibility in all directions. Then we got smart and decided we would lie down and roll in it instead of walking around in it and stomping it with our feet. The bamboo was sharp and one time a dried-out root that was protruding from the ground stabbed me in my stomach.

Yes, my time there was not easy.

Most of the enemy units broke up into small units to attack us. That made it difficult to spot them because they would shoot at us from the dense jungle. Much of the time you didn't really get to see who you were shooting at so we just sprayed the jungle with gunfire and aimed at rifle flashes. The only way you would know if you hit anyone was to go and do a body count, which we rarely did.

Like much of Southeast Asia, the weather in Vietnam is tropical and marked by a monsoon season. During that time of year, there were streams of trickling water that could turn into floods. One day our Navy Corpsman that traveled with us for medical care was crossing one of these streams and lost his footing and started to float away. You could see the fear in his eyes as he struggled to grab a branch and avoid being carried away by the moving stream. Everything turned out all right, but for several moments no one knew what was going to happen.

While I was in Vietnam a lot of the Marine Corps equipment was worn and antiquated. I don't know why, but that seemed to be the norm rather than the exception. I remember seeing helicopters that would leave the mountain or the hill that we were on, and they would actually fall first and then build up momentum to start flying. I always joked that the Marine Corps didn't give us new equipment because they thought we were going to destroy it in battle anyway.

At night we used a starlight scope for better night vision. It was just a round tube similar to a telescope. You peered through the starlight scope at night, and although everything looked green, you could actually see images. One night I picked the device up and looked through it and saw the enemy. It scared me because it also magnifies the image in the scope.

After being in Vietnam for a while and hearing rounds explode, you become familiar with the sounds and begin to distinguish between the various kinds of ammunition blowing up around you. I could tell what size the round was from the tone of the explosion. I knew whether it was a 60mm or 80mm or 122mm rocket or rifle fire. It became second nature. The AK-47 was one of the rifles that the enemy used, and it had a cracking sound similar to a whip. That rifle was a very good weapon because it could take a lot of punishment and still fire. It was a Russian or Chinese-made weapon. In contrast, we used an M-16 rifle, which required more attention. We had to be diligent and keep our rifle extra clean or it would jam.

In addition to being vigilant about the enemy, you also had to be keenly aware of what was happening around you. This included something called short rounds. When our mortar guys were firing at the enemy sometimes you would get rounds that didn't have enough explosive in it to propel them to the area where the gunner wanted them to go. These were called short rounds because they never made it to the intended target. They would just go straight up into the air and come straight down in the compound. When that happened, they would yell "short round," and when you hear that, you better run and scramble for the fox hole, because friendly fire or not, it still had the power to maim and kill.

My time in Vietnam was something I didn't talk about for years. I was proud to have served my country as a Marine in combat. Yet, when we got home we discovered that public perception was skewed and negative reports about the Vietnamese War were prevalent.

Consequently, you didn't want anyone to know you had been there. Also with post-traumatic stress disorder, one of the symptoms is not talking about what happened, so I probably had two things going on: first, the fear of talking about it and the actual stress it caused.

The post-traumatic stress affected me in ways I didn't recognize at first. I thought it was just my imagination. For example, after I got home from Vietnam I was at my mother's house visiting. There was a battery-powered clock on the wall in the room where I was sleeping, and the ticking reminded me of walking in Vietnam with a full pack. I could hear a clicking sound that just didn't seem to quit, so I got up and took the battery out of the clock. My family didn't understand and talked about me and my unusual behavior with comments like, "What's wrong with him? He's taking the battery out of the clocks and acting strange."

In talking with other veterans I have discovered that we all kept a lot of stuff inside because we were afraid that family and friends wouldn't understand us. Yet it was comforting that we were able to talk to other veterans about our situations and experiences with much more openness without fear of judgment or being misunderstood. That is exactly what goes on at the VA Hospital where I attended group therapy, and for the most part, we talked openly.

After being discharged from the Marine Corps for my wounds, I went back home to Sumter, South Carolina. I stayed there for a few weeks at my mother's house. Coming from Vietnam as a Marine, I felt too grown up to live with her for long. I needed to be out on my own, and before long I went to New York to live with my sister. I planned to stay there until I could get an apartment and find employment.

Being new to New York and looking for work, I remember my sister telling me, "If you ever get lost, don't come up out of the subway tunnel, because with all the streets and the tall buildings, you're bound to get confused." Her advice proved helpful as I began my quest to find a job.

One day I made my way over to the employment agency and was talking to a young lady there about finding work, but she didn't have anything for me. I left there and went to several other places but was still unsuccessful in my search. Finally, I went to a bank: Manufactures Hanover Trust Company. They had their personnel office on the premises, so I went in and talked to them. They hired me, and gave me a date to come in for a physical at the medical office. I went on the scheduled date and saw the doctor, who told me to strip down to my underwear and sit on the table, which I did. He saw my scars from Vietnam where I had been wounded: my right ankle, right thigh, middle right finger, and left shoulder. Early on, I used to bleed from my ears too because I was so close to the blast of the exploding 122mm rockets.

The doctor saw the scars and asked, "Where did you get those?"

My reluctance made me feel ashamed of myself because somehow the government had turned the war back on us and made us feel like it was our fault, even though I had volunteered to go. As I was silently bracing for words of rejection from the doctor, he looked at me and said, "If you're good enough to go to Vietnam, you're good enough to work here."

I couldn't believe my ears! I was so relieved and happy at the same time because I got treated in a very different manner. He hired me for the position.

That first job was at a large bank, and I worked on the 17th floor. I was excited about my new position, and I was eager to fit in. Picturing New York as a glamorous place, I started to buy clothes as soon as I could afford it so I could be properly dressed at my new job.

When I first moved to New York I wondered if I was dressing properly coming from South Carolina. I bought some clothes that I thought seemed more appropriate. They were probably the same clothes being worn in South Carolina, but my mind was telling me that people in New York would dress differently from those in my hometown.

One morning as I was walking up to the bank, there was a large stream of people walking with me because there were massive office buildings throughout the area. Just as I was a few steps away from the lobby of the bank, some workers outside started drilling in the street with a Milwaukee jackhammer. To me it sounded like a

50-caliber machine gun so I responded instinctively and got down on one knee. Seconds later I got up and was embarrassed because people were watching me. I didn't look to the left or the right. I just got up and went into my office building.

When I started at the bank, I was working in the quality control section. I was very naive, but a good worker because my mother had instilled a solid work ethic in me. My bosses liked my work, and eventually I was promoted to supervisor. Once I was promoted I had to deal with a lot of bosses located on the 10th floor. My self-esteem was very low, and I wasn't sure I had what it would take to succeed. To deal with my low self-esteem issues, my friend and I would go to a little deli nearby where we would have a couple of beers with lunch. When I came back from lunch, I felt empowered — as if I could talk to the world. This was *not* setting me up for success. Of course, I didn't realize this at the time.

Due to my low confidence issues, I doubted the quality of my work and expected to get a pink slip in my check every payday. In other words, "Don't come back to work!" I was young, naive, and very nervous about doing a good job.

I had changed from the way I grew up in South Carolina because of the war. I became increasingly angry, and was told by some of my co-workers at the bank, "Clarence, we can't even talk to you... you're so angry and ready to pounce on anybody for anything." By this time you couldn't get me near a church either because I think I was mad at God for Vietnam and the death of all my friends there...I just didn't understand the whole process.

I eventually worked myself up to the position of supervisor. My promotion helped me deal with my self-esteem issues, and I started to improve. At one time I briefly dated one of the vice presidents of a bank, but that didn't last long because I questioned whether or not I had what it took to date her so I walked away from that relationship. At some point while I was working at the bank, I decided to go to college using the G.I. Bill. The government gave us privileges, and I decided to use them.

During this period, I started reading the *New York Times*. I didn't know many of the words that were written in the paper, so I'd carry a dictionary with me and I would diligently study the words and write them down. Eventually, I didn't need the dictionary anymore because most of the words were repeated periodically. I was working to improve myself little by little.

I continued going to college and at some point I had an opportunity to apply with the fire department. I had a conflict with my college final exams because they were scheduled around the same time. I had to make a choice, so I took the exam with the fire department and didn't go back to take my final exams because I figured I would make the fire department my career.

One day, I was walking in Brooklyn and there were two firefighters in front of a firehouse passing out recruiting fliers to get guys into the New York City Fire Department. They handed me a flyer and said, "Why don't you come on in, take the test, and join the fire department?" I said to myself, "I'm having a lot of trouble in the streets. Maybe that would help me if I had a job doing tough stuff; maybe that would take some of the stress off me." Not knowing at the time that many war veterans look for similar jobs in either the police or the fire department because it's paramilitary—it's kind of an extension to being in the military and you can still act like you're on active duty. I took the flyer from the firefighters, but didn't have the money to file the application. So I borrowed the money from a friend and quickly filed the paperwork so I could take the test.

On the day of the exam, there were thousands of people there. I couldn't believe how many guys had shown up. In addition, there were several other schools around town where the test was also being given. With thousands of men at this one location I thought to myself, "I don't stand a chance." I started to walk away because I wanted to go drink...an emotional crutch I had begun leaning on in the Marine Corps, and one that was becoming all too familiar, especially when faced with an obstacle.

As I began walking away, that familiar voice came to me and said, "Clarence, you're already here. Just stay and take the test." I didn't hesitate. I turned around, went inside and took the test. I was in the 2nd class to be assigned to the FDNY. I could never have imagined where and what that decision would lead to in the years ahead.

Chapter Fourteen - The Man in the Mirror, the Boy of Yesterday

We plan our lives according to a dream that comes to us in our childhoods and then life alters our plans.
~Ben Okri

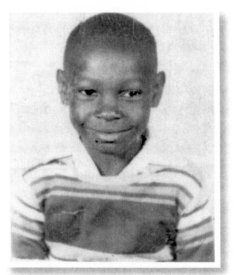

In the second grade in Sumter, S.C.

When I think back, I'm amazed at the defining events in my adult life that I have been a part of. Of course the lessons I learned from those experiences—Vietnam, World Trade Center Bombing, 9/11—made me the man I am today. So I often wonder how I ended up in those places. Growing up, I had no indication of what was in store of me as an adult.

I was born in 1949 and there were ten of us living in a four-room house, which consisted of a living room that doubled as my parents' bedroom, a kitchen, and two bedrooms. The seventh of eight children, I had four sisters and three brothers. The four boys slept in the same bed, with two sleeping at the head of the bed and two at the foot. My four sisters shared the other bedroom and slept in a bed just like we did: two at the head of the bed and two at the foot.

Although we were quite poor, we still lived by a very strict moral code. My mother took us to Sunday School class and taught us the difference between right and wrong. She was a very hard worker. I have never seen a woman that worked as much as my mother did. She would start before the sun came up and continue late into the evening. She kept going day after day and year after year. She always told us to work for what you want, and she actually lived that example for us. She told us not to steal and stressed the importance of being kind to people.

We never had any locks on our doors, because in our community no one stole anything from anyone. When leaving the house we would just close the front door and go. Toys and other items could be left in the yard and they were still there when you returned to play with them again.

We used wood and coal stoves for heating and cooking. I spent many days in the woods cutting fuel for the fire. Coal was purchased at one of the local stores. Kerosene lamps were used to light our house. I remember when our home was finally wired for electricity, and we were able to use real lights instead of kerosene lamps. As you can imagine, it was very exciting and much less work for us to have electric lights and heat!

Our house didn't have city water either, so a long metal hollow pole was driven into the ground until it reached water. A hand pump was attached to the top of the pole to cause suction to be created, forcing water to come to the surface. There were no city sewage services in our home either. Our toilet was a wooden structure behind the house approximately four-feet wide and six-feet tall, placed over a hole in the ground.

We did not have a telephone in our house during those days. If we needed to make a call, we would go to someone else's house to use the phone. The people that were fortunate enough to have a phone usually had a party line; that meant they actually had to share one phone line with approximately five other households. If you picked up the receiver and heard voices talking, you were out of luck. Someone else was already using the line and you had to wait your turn. Of course as precocious kids we would sometimes get a thrill out of listening in on someone else's conversation, that is, until our mother found out!

Owning a television was even more rare than having a telephone. One of our neighbors had a TV and all of the local children would go there to watch programs as often as they would allow. At that time, only black and white TVs existed. There was no such thing as full-color televisions. I remember at some point a screen with visible green, red, and blue lines could be purchased and placed over the TV screen to give the appearance of a color set.

With no television except at the neighbor's house, we made the most of our toys, using whatever was available. For example, I remember creating some stilts by hammering a short piece of wood about two feet from the bottom of a longer piece. We would also take a hanger and use it to roll old bicycle rims. By tacking bottle caps to the bottoms of our shoes we could make taps for tap dancing. Life was simple. We had a way of having fun by doing things like playing football, running through the fields at night playing hide and seek, and playing marbles. Back then, the outdoors was our internet!

My mother was a very strong woman and the disciplinarian of the family. Mother was reared by her grandmother, because her mother died when she was just a girl. According to the stories my mother told us, her grandmother was also very strict so I guess it ran in the family. Mother said there came a time when she could not take the punishment anymore so she ran away and caught a bus and came to Sumter, South Carolina. I've done research, and it appears that my great-grandmother was a slave, which is not surprising given when she was alive. I can only imagine how that kind of a life affected her and many thousands of others, and that may have contributed to her surly nature. However, in my family my mother was the enforcer, and I am sure that the way she treated us was a direct result of the way that she was treated as a child.

Eventually my great-grandmother came to live with one of my relatives on Foxworth Street in Sumter, one block behind Williams Street, the street we lived on. I have very little memory of her, but I do recall my older relatives saying that she walked with a cane and would use the hook to put around the neck of anyone that she wanted to punish, pulling them over to her.

As the primary disciplinarian in the family, mother had a unique style. If we misbehaved, she wouldn't punish us immediately. Rather, she would say, "When I get you, I am going to get you for the old and the new." The anticipation made the punishment much worse because you never knew when your time would run out and judgment would fall. When judgment day finally arrived, my mother would beat us seemingly for a long time. She would beat us so hard that on many occasions I went to school with marks on my arms and back. The waiting and constant uncertainty of when her discipline would be administered set in motion the feeling of impending doom, which spilled over into my adult life and haunted me on the job, fearing that I would suddenly be terminated from the position.

Under the circumstances, my mother did the best that she could do, considering the way she was disciplined as a child. I don't think my mother was aware that her disciplinary style had this effect on us. It was the only way she knew to raise a family. In addition to low self-esteem issues, her treatment of us may have affected my relationships with others in my adult life. It took years for me to deal with this and put it behind me so I could have better relationships with women.

I was the only one of my mother's children that would work in the fields, rake yards, and do other odd jobs and bring the money I earned home and give it to her. Being the disciplinarian my mother was, I could never understand why she would beat me with electric cords, limbs from trees or anything she could get her hands on when I was giving her so much and trying to help out in any way I could.

My father, on the other hand, was a very kind and soft-spoken man. He punished us on occasion, but his beatings were not as severe as my mother's. Once he had one of my older sisters in a room and we heard what sounded like a terrible beating coming from behind the closed door. Each time we heard the swat, a corresponding scream with intense crying would follow. However, when someone opened the door to the room, we learned that he was hitting the bed and my sister was pretending to be crying. That was our entertainment!

As long as I can remember, I have always loved rocking chairs. From the time I was a child I would rock myself to sleep. When a rocking chair was not available, I would improvise, banging myself against the back of a regular table chair, causing the front legs to lift off of the floor giving me the sense of rocking. Because we had wood floors in our house the neighbors could hear me banging the chair over and over. One of the quickest ways to get me angry was to try to stop me from rocking or bumping my chair.

My mother and older siblings told me about a time when I was sitting in the straight-back chair banging it back and forth while my mother was cooking in the kitchen. As I rocked back and forth, I folded my arms and said, "Hurry up and give me one of those g-d d-n biscuits!" On another occasion my mother was cooking hog chitterlings and I am told that I said, "Those things smell like s- - t."

I don't know where those words came from, and what is unusual about this is during those days children wouldn't dare use profanity around adults. If they did they were beaten, but my mother only laughed at what I said. Until this very day (and I am now in my sixties) my family still jokes about these two incidences. Some of my sisters have said, "If anyone other than Clarence had said these things, they would have been punished."

My mother and father separated when I was in grade school. He started seeing a lady that lived on the same street as we did. My father rented a room in a boarding house in our neighborhood, and on Friday evenings my siblings and I would go visit him to get our weekly allowance. In those days a dime went a long way. Large cookies were two for a penny, and you could get into the movies for ten cents.

I could never understand some relationships in Sumter because it was known that husbands, wives, girlfriends and boyfriends would have affairs and everyone in the community was aware of it, including the person that was being cheated on. What is odd about these types of affairs is it seemed to me to have been accepted. In some cases the person would spend hours or days with their lover and return home with little or nothing said.

When my father left the house I was just a kid, but I took on his responsibilities and started taking care of my mother. Without being asked, I would always rake the yard, mop the floors, and clean the house when my mother was away. I liked the nice comments that she would give me when she returned. Perhaps this was when the rescuer within me began to emerge because although I was a child, I started helping my mother and others at a very early age when the other kids were playing and having fun. On many occasions I would tell myself that when I got married I would never leave my wife for another woman or for any other reason. Sadly, that would not be the case. I did not realize it at the time, but taking care of my mother at such an early age was the beginning of a life helping women that spilled over into my adult life and resulted in some hurtful relationships.

During those days if a neighbor saw you doing something questionable, it was surely going to get back to your parents. It was as if the entire community was there to discipline the children. Fortunately, none of my brothers or sisters ever got into any type of trouble with the law. All of us had jobs and took care of ourselves, even though some were not as productive as others. We had quarrels like most families do, but we were basically a tight knit group perhaps because of our difficult upbringing. We learned to rely on ourselves and each other.

Chapter Fourteen – The Man in the Mirror, the Boy of Yesterday

We grew up during the time when it was accepted for parents to have a lot of children so they could work in fields such as picking cotton and vegetables. I didn't complain about the hard work, but sometimes I felt embarrassed. I didn't like it when we were working in the cotton fields alongside the highways, and people from the North would stop and take pictures of us.

There were many times when I was kept out of school to work in the fields, and it was uncomfortable for me because after being absent for an extended period of time, I had to face my classmates upon my return to school. This would happen repeatedly throughout the school year. In spite of missing my classes, I was always able to catch up with the lesson that the other students were on. In the face of this difficult situation, it's hard to believe I never failed a class.

As field workers we were trucked to the farm early in the mornings before the sun rose, and since none of the passersby were able to see me, I was okay with being on the trucks. In the evening after toiling in the hot sun all day, I tried to get as near to the back of the truck as possible, so that I would not be called a "cotton picker" by people we passed on our way back home. I was ashamed because of the type work that we were doing, but at least it was honest labor. The trucks would make several stops dropping people at their houses. It seemed to me that the children that did not have to work in the fields were better than I was.

I saw myself as a tough young man during my preteen and teenage years. One day as we were working in the field picking cotton some of the older girls coerced me into fighting an older guy. He laced into me without waiting for me to take the first swing. He would pick me up and throw me down onto the powdery white sand so hard that it practically created a dust storm. It looked like he was tossing me into a barrel of flour. Still, I kept going back because I didn't want the girls to think I was afraid to defend myself.

Growing up, I was basically a quiet, stay-at-home kid. One night some of the local boys who were apparently feeling mischievous jumped on top of an old model-T Ford that was owned by an elderly reverend and they started banging on it. Later, when the reverend told the story in his deep voice he said, "Those boys jumped on my car and bang, bang...there was the hole, but I know one of them was Clarence Singleton." I was nowhere near the site when the incident took place. Until this day when I see any of my friends from that era, they sometimes say with a smile, "I know one of them was Clarence Singleton."

After a law was enacted to keep children in school and out of the fields, I found jobs working in restaurants part-time. I worked in a variety of positions. I was a dishwasher, a bus boy clearing tables and taking dirty dishes to the kitchen, and I even worked at a restaurant that had curb service. This is when you go to the car and take the order. When the order was ready, the cashier called your number, and then you would go inside, get the food, and bring it to the car. The hourly pay from the owner was minimal, but the tips we were given made up the difference.

For the most part whites patronized the restaurants; so on occasions fights would start when we would be called a derogatory name. We would watch to see if a car was going to turn into the lot of the restaurant from the street, and the first person that said the name of the car would get to serve the customer.

One night I said the name of a car, which meant that it was my customer, but one of the older and bigger guys took the car from me. When he went inside to place the order, I noticed that he was sitting on a wooden soda crate. As payback I took a nail and forced it into his seat...sharp point up. When he came back and sat down, he jumped up screaming and holding his backside. He said, "I know Clarence put the nail in my seat," but he couldn't prove it.

During my middle school years I worked at a fruit and vegetable market located in downtown Sumter at the foot of a bridge that spanned the railroad tracks. When the shelves and bins were low on items I would restock them from a walk-in refrigerator, as well as help sell and bag the items for the customer. Several days each week we would load the truck and the boss lady, who we called "little lady" because she was small in stature, would drive to residential areas and we would peddle or sell fruits and vegetables. When the inventory was low she would take us to Columbia, South Carolina to a large market to purchase more goods. I had a crush on my boss, so when she started dating a fellow, I was devastated. Because of my feelings for her it eventually caused me to be fired, because I did not want to take orders from her boyfriend.

During the summer months, owners of tobacco fields would come to our neighborhood looking for people to go stay on their farms to help take the tobacco from the fields and put it into barns for curing. If you decided to go, you would stay on the farm anywhere from four to six weeks. I was in my teens when I begged my mother to let me go to the farm to work. She finally gave me permission, and I happily got on the truck and left.

Working in the tobacco fields was quite an experience. It was always hot and the tobacco was gummy. Girls and younger boys would work at the barn tying the tobacco to sticks so the bigger guys could hang them in the barns for curing. When hanging the tobacco in the barns one guy would climb rafters to the top of the barn, another guy would position himself in the middle, and the third worker would stop near the bottom of the rafters. Hanging green tobacco wasn't as bad as taking cured tobacco out of the barns; when it was removed from the barns, it had dried, and the sand and little pieces of broken tobacco would get into your eyes, nose and mouth. When the job was done, we would be covered with dust and debris. With the money that I made from this and the other jobs that I had, I used it to buy clothes and books for school. Yet, sometimes there was still a shortage of money, and we had to make do with what we had.

There were many days when I did not have shoes to wear to school and in some cases my shoes had holes in the bottom. I would cut a piece of cardboard to cover the hole, which kept my feet from touching the ground, but on rainy days the cardboard disintegrated and I would end up with a soggy foot! Although we sometime did not have enough food or decent clothes to wear, my mother always washed the clothes that we had and kept us clean.

As we got older, there were about three clubs that we would go to on Friday and Saturday nights to dance and have fun. I was not a drinker or a good dancer. I would have a cup in my hand, pretending that I had alcohol in it, but that was far from the truth. Every now and then someone would start a fight in the club, but when the fight was over, it was over. No one went to jail or got a lawyer to sue the offender.

It's probably very hard for most people to imaging growing up in a time when segregation was accepted as normal behavior. Even though it was difficult, it was all we knew at the time. Blacks and whites never dined together in the same restaurant. There were three movie theaters in town. Two of them were segregated, which meant the whites went to one theater and the blacks went to another. The third theater had two floors. The upper balcony was where blacks could view the movie, although they had to enter the theater through the alley. The larger area on the first floor of the theater was reserved for anyone who was white. There were even separate concession stands with fewer items for sale for the blacks over the variety of concessions available on the lower level for the whites. A black man could be jailed or beaten if he was caught looking at a white woman, let alone date one. The police always took the side of the whites; it made no difference if they were right or wrong.

Segregation even applied to public water fountains, which were designated for either black or white folks. If you were black you also had to ride in the back of the city buses. The way we were treated made me feel inferior to other races. It took a lot of work for me to overcome these feelings, but I have made progress in that area. There are times when I still do self-talk to overcome negative and self-oppressive thinking.

I remember an incident when my brother, my cousin and I were walking through a white neighborhood and this white guy who was a boxer and a tough guy ran over and started fighting us. If we had defended ourselves, we would have still been in the wrong because that was just the way it was.

On another occasion I was caught by the police with a hunting knife and was promptly arrested. When my lawyer came to get me out of jail, he would not accept any money from me. He said that I should not have been incarcerated in the first place for the offense, but it was just a sign of the times.

A few days after the Civil Rights Act became law, a few of my friends and I went into an all-white restaurant with the idea that we would finally be welcomed. However, it was just the opposite. We were humiliated and rudely asked to get out, since we were outnumbered, we left. It was a long time to come before I dared to try that again.

In the 1980s, I drove a few teenage African Americans to a community dance in Sumter. When we arrived I was shocked and happy to see that both Caucasians and African Americans were socializing at the same dance. I had been living in New York since 1969 and did not realize that the relationship between the two groups had changed for the better in my hometown. At that moment, although my mind was still stuck in the past as far as the South was concerned, I realized that the South had changed and it was a new day!

Chapter Fifteen — Facing the Demons

It is better to conquer yourself than to win a thousand battles.
~Buddha

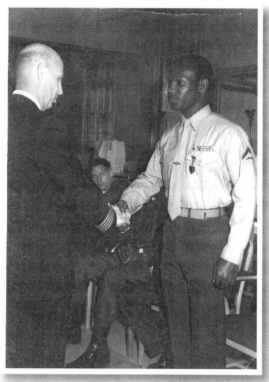

*Clarence receives the Purple Heart for being wounded in action
in the Vietnam War.*

Raised by a woman with an iron fist, I behaved myself. But I started drinking when I was in the Marine Corps in Vietnam. At first, it was just something to do with the guys, and it didn't have much of an effect on me. I was able to function without any problems. I'm sure things would have gotten progressively worse if I was not wounded and had not gotten an early discharge.

After I got home and as time went on, it seemed as if a drink now and then helped me cope with life. Later as a husband and as a firefighter my drinking caused lots of problems directly and indirectly. I wasn't paying the monthly bills, and I wasn't being a good father to my children. It was more important to me to spend the money on drinking and partying. My wife was forced to shoulder the responsibility and kept the family together as best she could. She bought clothes for the boys, made sure they were in good schools, and were fed properly.

I was keeping up with my responsibilities at work and doing my job at the fire department, but I did have to take days off now and then because I was hung over from drinking. There were days that I did manage to go to work when I was not feeling well. On those days I would pride myself for being able to show up after drinking most of the night. The pride of me going to work on these days was detrimental because it blocked out the times that I could not go to the firehouse and made it difficult for me to see that I had a problem.

Soon I was drinking more and more, and it became a means by which I could self-medicate and forget the painful memories that haunted me from Vietnam. Before I realized it, my drinking had a hold on me that I couldn't shake off, and eventually I was arrested. At first, the police officers would give me a little slap on the wrist and tell me to stay out of trouble. Being the strong, tough former-Marine that I was, I thought I could handle it, so I didn't heed their admonitions.

My drinking problem crept up on me subtly, and I found myself making more and more bad decisions. In no time at all I was arrested again for drinking. This particular time I had broken the window out of my wife's car. Following my arrest I was in the jail cell and I was lying there looking around telling myself I was going to find a way to escape. I didn't have any tools or anything, but I kept thinking to myself there has to be a weak spot in here, and I'm gonna find it and get out.

I could hear the two police officers talking in the room next to me. They were discussing my situation. Moments later the sound of the voices in the next room faded to nothing as one of them peeked around the wall to get a glimpse of me. The puzzled expression on his face seemed to say, "This is a firefighter? Acting like this? He needs to get his act together."

Because I was in the fire department, they allowed my sister's boyfriend to come back to the cell to visit me. I was happy to see him, but not because I wanted any visitors. In a whisper, I asked him to run an errand for me. I told him to go to McDonald's, buy a soda, and pour it out; then go to the liquor store, fill it up with ice and alcohol, and bring it back to me. How could I not see I had a problem?

He did exactly as I had requested, and when he returned, they allowed him to come back to my cell. I'm not sure if they looked in the cup before they allowed him back in the jail, but he came in to see me with the alcohol. As soon as he handed me the cup from McDonald's, I took another drink. I didn't want to feel; I just wanted to numb myself.

I didn't break out of the cell as I had contemplated when they locked me up. I got out when they took the key and opened the door for me to leave. I was grateful that all I got was time to sober up and a warning not to get in trouble again. That day as I was released from the jail, I walked out of there thinking I was a free man when I was actually imprisoned by the power that alcohol had over me.

During this period my wife was suffering because I was doing these things to her, and there were never any consequences from the law. It was a very difficult situation for her because she was hurting, and no one could see her pain. We finally made up and I made amends to my wife. After everything that we have been through, even our divorce, we are friends today. She is the mother to my children, and I am grateful she and I have worked through the pain to where we are cordial and pleasant to each other again.

However, at the time, my drinking was escalating, but it was so subtle that I did not realize that I was causing so much pain. Finally one of my officers sent me to rehab after my wife called and complained about me and the problems that my drinking was causing.

Just prior to going into rehab, I was driving my wife's car. We were going up to the daycare to pick up one of our sons. We were living separately at the time, and I found out she was seeing someone. As I was driving along I was thinking about crashing the car into some cars that were parallel parked on the street on her side, but then I changed my mind. Instead I purposely drove through a busy intersection against a red light, and miraculously no cars were coming. When that didn't work, I spun the car around and crashed it into a church fence. As soon as the car came to a halt, I got out and threw her keys into the bushes in someone's yard. For a split second it was like a door opening in my mind saying, "Clarence, you weren't always this way. What's going on?" But just as quickly as that door to my thoughts opened, the door closed again and I went on doing the same things. That's when my wife called the fire department and said, "Can't you see Clarence is having a problem with his drinking?" Her call for help started things in motion.

The fire department finally told me that if I got into any more trouble, I was going to rehab. I continued to make unwise choices, and before long I found myself in rehab. Just like the fire department warned me.

During this period, I was also studying for my lieutenant's test and all the guys that I was studying with called the counselor and told him the test was right around the corner, adding, "Clarence is the best student. Why don't you let him out of rehab so he can take the test?"

However, the system had rules, and they wouldn't budge. The guys didn't give up. They kept calling on my behalf, and finally the fire department's counseling service unit said they'd let me out to take the test, adding that I had to return to finish up my treatment as soon as I had taken the exam.

I got out of rehab and continued studying with the guys. The night before I was to take the test I went to my wife's house and got into an argument, which resulted in my being arrested once again. The officer on duty found out I was a firefighter and had to take a test the next day so he rushed me through the system. I was able to take the exam, but got into trouble again. The fire department had modified their policy and let me out of the treatment program, and my actions violated the trust they had put in me. Because of my situation, they changed the rules for a while and said they were no longer going to let guys out of the rehab treatment program once they had begun treatment.

After taking the lieutenant's test and being discharged from the hospital, I went to the firehouse to get my check. My face was battered so I stayed in the car because I felt so embarrassed and ashamed. I remember the captain coming out to give me my check. He had never seen me like this before, and I knew he could tell how I was doing just by looking at me.

During this period, I was in a great deal of pain. There were lots of signs that I had changed, but I didn't know the cause. On one or two occasions I saw reports on the news about a Marine and other military personnel in Texas who had lost it and were holed up in a tower shooting people in the street below. I feared that I might become just like that. I used to go to my spiritual groups, and the other people would be there laughing and having fun. As I watched from the sidelines I often thought, "How can they laugh and be so happy when I'm in so much pain?" Later I learned through experience that when I can laugh at myself after going through something painful, it's a sign that I'm growing emotionally. I discovered that sharing about emotional pain cuts the problem in half.

I was trying to put my life back together. I would share things at my spiritual group. Then after the meeting I would call my wife because I wanted to get back together with her. I would tell her about what I had learned or heard at the meeting, assuring her that I had changed. No matter what I said or did, she was not convinced. I've learned since that time that trust comes back by doing right things over a period of time, and in some cases, it may not come back at all. Trust is earned gradually; it cannot be bestowed on someone just by making a decision.

Trust is not just words. Trust is action. You can speak a great deal about what you've learned, but you have to prove things by what you do. Day in and day out I had blown the chance to prove I could be a new man with my wife.

Still, I just continued making better choices and doing right things and at a point my wife wanted to get back with me. In the end, however, we never rekindled our romance, but our relationship got better, and I made amends to my wife. We have been through a lot, and after everything, I am happy that we have a healthy, friendly relationship now. She understands the situation I was in with the drinking because she recognized that I had changed. I have always respected her because she's the mother of my children, and she has done a tremendous job. We get along very well today, and for that I'm grateful. Sometimes, a couple goes through so many profound experiences that they can't quite repair what was once there. That was the case with us. But the respect remains.

After being put in my spiritual program, I completely stopped drinking. When I went back to full duty at my company, 12 Truck, I made amends to my captain. He responded with such kindness, saying, "Oh, Clarence, it's no problem. I wish I had a company of men just like you." Those understanding words made me feel really good. I guess what I felt was the goodness of God for what I've come through and where I am now. After the captain said that to me, it helped me let go of some of the past. Finally I could move forward. Part of my spiritual program is about making amends.

But, one of the people I needed to make amends to was me. I needed to forgive myself for the mistakes I had made. I needed to forgive myself for the post-traumatic stress disorder I suffered from that caused me to make some very bad decisions.

Sadly, everyone did not respond in the same manner as my captain. There was another lieutenant in the firehouse I decided to apologize to. I went back to make amends to him, and told him I apologized. He didn't say anything so I thought maybe he didn't hear me, so I said it again. He didn't respond the second time either, so I thought, "Well, I've done what I have to do and he can be any way that he wants. I made the amends and it's up to him if he accepts it or not." It would have been more pleasant if he had accepted my apology, but I had freed myself. I had taken responsibility for my actions, and that's all I can do. This is a lesson I have carried with me. In life, today, I make amends when things happen, rather than let things fester. But that doesn't mean the person I make amends to will accept it right away. That's okay. It is about being at peace with myself.

As I was continuing with my recovery, I still had the calling to be the rescuer. In August of 2005, Hurricane Katrina brought her deadly fury to New Orleans to create one of the most horrific natural disasters of our time. When I heard about it, I immediately sensed the call of duty and wanted to respond. I found out that a few other veterans from the VA Hospital in Brooklyn were calling some of the therapists at the VA Hospital asking, "Is Clarence going down to New Orleans?" I really wanted to go, and we were actually making preparations by trying to find a fire department unit that was headed in that direction so that we could travel with them.

Something tugged at my heart with such intensity. I knew there were so many desperate people waiting for someone to help, and I longed to do what I could. At the same time, however, I wasn't the most likely candidate; I was suffering from post-traumatic stress and depression. My ankle hurt from my injuries in Vietnam, and my right shoulder was sore from being injured at the Twin Towers on 9/11. One of the other firefighters was also struggling with his own health issues. He had suffered an injury to his ankle on the job, and that was causing him great pain. Our minds were made up though, and we were determined to go down to New Orleans to help.

However, when my therapist got wind of what we were planning to do, she said, "No. You guys aren't going anywhere. It's like a war zone down there, and you really don't need to see that stuff." That put a damper on our rescue plans, and though disheartened, we finally recognized the wisdom of the therapist's words and canceled our trip.

In retrospect I know my therapist was right. I thought about it afterwards, and there probably wasn't much we could have done to help in light of the injuries we all were dealing with at the time. I wasn't able to work much and neither were the other guys. The sense of responsibility I felt was strong, and even though I was not able to go, it showed me the drive and passion that I have in me to help people when duty calls.

With the wisdom of hindsight, I have come to realize that when I put all my trust in God, things work out for me. I don't have to carry around the heavy weight that once burdened me down every moment of the day. I still have times when I feel the weight of past memories and experiences, but in those times—whether it's on a daily basis or even an hourly basis—I give it to Him and He's always there to lift my burden if I just surrender it to Him.

Chapter Sixteen — Trying to Forget

We each need to make peace with our own memories.
We have all done things that make us flinch.
~Surya Das

Clarence on the job as a firefighter.

After the collapse, some of the firefighters from Engine 218, the company I retired from, called me and told me that there were some pictures of me in a studio in lower Manhattan. I went over to the studio where a photographer had a number of photos on display from the World Trade Center and 9/11. I saw my pictures exhibited on the wall along with many others. After some time, I introduced myself and let him know that I was in some of his photographs. They were good quality, and he was selling them. However, he gave me mine free of charge. He said for anyone who was at the site, he was giving them their pictures at no cost. One of them that he was offering for sale was priced at $50. He told me that when he was at the site he thought he had only taken a couple pictures, but when he developed them, he discovered that he had taken hundreds. Probably the shock of the day made it all a blur.

That's the thing about the tricky mind. During trauma, some things are a blur. Some are crystal clear.

Apparently something similar happened to him as what I experienced that day at the base of the North Tower. My brain wouldn't allow me to comprehend what was going on down there as the Tower was collapsing and people were fleeing the area. It's a defense mechanism.

While I was in the photo gallery looking at the pictures, I noticed some pictures of people standing on the upper floors of the World Trade Center. At least one guy had his arms folded, and he looked like he was ready to jump. There were even some pictures of people leaping from some of the top floors of North Tower, and their bodies looked like they were suspended in mid-air in the photos. I had visited the observation deck of the World Trade Center on several occasions. Based on that experience, I know what kind of perspective those people had that day. Their decision to jump must have been one of total desperation and a sense of utter hopelessness. I like to think that people of faith made a choice to meet their God with a sense of peace in the midst of a horrendous nightmare.

It's still very difficult for me to think about. I can only imagine what they went through as the smoke was rising around them and they realized they had two choices: burn or jump.

On several occasions I've tried to recall other building collapses that I've worked at while I was in the fire department because that's something firefighters often do. Yet every time I try to think of one, the World Trade Center comes to the forefront and kinda washes all the others out of my thoughts. I have to keep going back in my memory as a mental exercise, trying to get the World Trade Center out of my mind as I try to remember the other collapses that I was at in an attempt to balance what happened on 9/11 with all the other rescues and life experiences from my firefighting days and my time in Vietnam.

Even to this day, almost anything can trigger thoughts of 9/11. Sometimes when I'm watching TV or if I'm outside and see dust, I think of the World Trade Center because of all the dust that was around during the collapse of the Towers. My thoughts can be totally on something else, and suddenly a sound or an object or something will ambush my mind and carry me back to some detail related to 9/11.

One day, I was in my living room, lying on the couch talking to a friend on the telephone. Over my fireplace in my TV room I have a 50-inch flat screen TV. As my friend and I were talking, I just happened to look over to my left, and at the exact moment that I glanced in that direction, the collapse of the North Tower was being replayed on the television. Even though I was in my home, the size of my TV and the picture of the collapsing Tower in high-definition made it all so real to me again that I screamed out loud. I could see the Tower and the antenna on the roof...such familiar sights...and the whole thing was collapsing before my eyes again!

My friend on the phone asked, "What's going on?"

I told him what had happened and realized it was only a flashback. Yet, for me in that moment, it was happening again.

I still have these moments from time to time. Some people have a misunderstanding of what flashbacks are. They are usually associated with veterans that have been to war who are haunted by memories of battle. Thoughts of being at a traumatic scene or event are not really flashback. A flashback is when you feel as if you are actually at the scene and see yourself at a particular event again as you experience the trauma and emotion of that event all over again.

That's what happened to me that day when I saw the collapse of the World Trade Center on my TV. For a split second, I was there, and the fear and sense of impending danger was present with all the fury of 9/11. It was horrible and as real to me as when it happened.

I still try not to look at pictures of the World Trade Center and the collapse, but sometimes when I'm watching TV, it's hard to avoid. This was especially true when the ten-year anniversary was approaching. It's possible that the feelings may always be with me, but I'm trying to learn how to manage them differently...one day at a time.

Things that can trigger a flashback include crowds, sirens, elevators, a certain smell of burning gasoline, the roar of a jet, even the sky being just so on a September day.

I can still have times of self-imposed isolation because of the experiences I've had. When that happens, I usually force myself to go out and be with people. Sometimes I like to choose the people that I share certain things with. I think that everyone means well, but some people have told me to "suck it up." Others have said, "Get over your feelings and go on with life." I wish it was as simple as that because I would love to leave it all behind me and go on with my life. They don't understand what I'm going through or what others may be going through. Usually, the guys that understand the best are the people who have been in the military and have been to war. They have a deeper understanding of what a fellow veteran actually sees and hears in combat.

When I finally got to Virginia after I relocated, I began participating in a group therapy session at the VA hospital in Richmond. Initially, I was again very reluctant to talk about the World Trade Center in a group session, thinking that the guys didn't want to hear it. However, all of my reluctance was just my unwarranted fears because it never came true. In fact, it was just the opposite.

The VA heroes respected me. They were very friendly and never said one negative thing about what I shared. They supported me and wanted to hear stories of what happened to me at the World Trade

Center site, which was also part of the healing process for me. On a few occasions, we ventured beyond the group setting and went fishing together. It was a very positive thing because we had a nice day of fishing, talking, and laughing. I have discovered that it's a plus to hang out with other veterans because often they are going through many of the same feelings so they understand. You can share things with them that some people who haven't been to war may not be able to relate to.

Once, when I went to the VA Hospital in Brooklyn, I spoke to a therapist. She probed a bit and gave me something to think about. She was a nurse practitioner named Barbara. I was sitting at her desk and I remember her asking me a question I had never been asked before—one that made me stop and think for several minutes. She asked, "When was the last time you were happy?" I didn't know how to respond or what to say because I couldn't remember the last time I actually felt happy. The only instance I could come up with was when I got a bicycle when I was a kid growing up in South Carolina. Sadly, that was the only happy memory I could recall.

Barbara was a well-respected nurse practitioner at the VA Hospital, and it didn't take long at all for me to realize that Barbara was a perfect choice for her position. She once took a trip to Vietnam to really get to feel and see what her veterans endured. Barbara spoke of some of the trails that she walked and could see how they can conceal the enemy and cause fear in the grunts or infantry men. We've talked many times that we're going to be sorry when she retires, but we also know that day is coming. She told me some things about how veterans respond and behave because of being in Vietnam. It seemed as if she had been to war because she described all the things that I was going through.

For example, sometimes when it rains my mind goes back to Vietnam. What she shared reminded me of feelings I still deal with: waking at night, going over to the windows and looking out when it's dark to check the perimeter. I can't sit in front of windows at night if the curtains or blinds are open because I feel like there might be a sniper out there and my head is going to explode from his bullet. Until I spoke with Barbara, I thought I was the only one who ever experienced feelings like that. I didn't know other guys were suffering from the same things I was experiencing. I just thought it was normal for me to have these thoughts.

At one point Barbara interviewed several guys with the intention of forming a special group. It was a very unique approach, and all the guys loved her for doing it. We were all firefighters, all of us were in Vietnam and some were at the World Trade Center site. I was comfortable with the group and could talk about anything, be it Vietnam, the fire department or something in my personal life. Regardless of what the topic was, I knew I could talk about it because all the guys had experienced this in some manner also. I was grateful to have at least one group that I could go to and talk about any of these monumental influences in my life.

On more than one occasion I have experienced the same thing in group sessions. If I'm with a regular group of civilians who were not in Vietnam and I talk about Vietnam or the fire department, some of them didn't like it and became uncomfortable. However, this was not the case in Barbara's group. We could talk about anything in the group Barbara formed, and I enjoyed that.

As a matter of fact, in this group there was a firefighter who was on the job when I joined Engine 55 in lower Manhattan. He trained me, and we met up later in this group at the VA Hospital. I learned that he had a son on the job, and he was at the World Trade Center site. He was worrying about his son and hoping that he was okay. We also had a chief in the group who had lost a son at the World Trade Center site. It was a bonding moment and an important part of my recovery.

Chapter Seventeen - New Beginnings

In all things it is better to hope than to despair.
~Johann von Goethe

Clarence and Mary Jean Singleton, 9/11/2012.

I got remarried in 2012 and it was like the plot of a movie or TV show—a retired fire lieutenant meets and falls madly in love with a superintendent forensic chemist!

To be honest, as soon as I met my wife, I knew she was special, but we had a long-distance relationship at first—and we all know how those usually turn out.

But something about us was different. I had a strong feeling that this was right and that we would eventually be married. And if that isn't a sign of the hope of a new life, I don't know what is. If I had to put my finger on it, I would say that we have both matured to the point where we put God first.

All my life, in my other relationships, no matter how mature I pretended to be, there was always a selfish element present. That wasn't the case with my new wife and me. And once we decided to get married, there was another important decision to make. We had to choose a date.

When I asked Mary Jean to marry me we both decided to pray on what date to choose for this important event. This is part of my new life now. I ask God what He intends instead of me putting my foot down and telling Him what I want.

But as I prayed, the date I kept hearing was September 11. That may seem perfectly logical to other people because of my involvement, but for me it was just the opposite. At first it seemed like a very bad idea. In fact, I just thought I had finally lost it. *Clarence,* I told myself, *that is the craziest thing ever.*

But Mary Jean, my sweet and wonderful wife and best friend, had been praying and the date she kept hearing in her prayerful heart was September 11. And as coincidence would have it, that also happens to be her birthday!

Both of us kept this from each other. When we sat down to plan the wedding, I think she mentioned it first, but we both blurted out "September 11th."

When I thought about it, our wedding date would be the eleventh anniversary of the fall of the Twin Towers. So that September 11th date was swirling all around us. Her birthday, the 11th anniversary, September 11th itself, it was all too much to ignore. But I still, to be honest, wanted to argue with God. You would think by now I would know better.

No matter how much I argued in my mind, God was a lot more powerful than I was. After a while, I sat alone with my thoughts and considered it.

Why was getting married on September 11th so important? Getting married on September 11th at 11:00 a.m. was about making a bold statement and that's something I was learning to do. I've learned to talk about my past, face my demons, even write about all that I've experienced.

Love is stronger than hate. It is stronger than racism. It is stronger than the bonds of slavery and poverty.

Love is stronger than the terrorists who struck American soil.

Love is stronger than evil. It is stronger than religious intolerance.

Love, as 1 Corinthians 13 tells us . . .

If I speak in the tongues[i] of men or of angels, but do not have love, I am only a resounding gong or a clanging cymbal. If I have the gift of prophecy and can fathom all mysteries and all knowledge, and if I have a faith that can move mountains, but do not have love, I am nothing. If I give all I possess to the poor and give over my body to hardship that I may boast, but do not have love, I gain nothing.

Love is patient, love is kind. It does not envy, it does not boast, it is not proud. It does not dishonor others, it is not self-seeking, it is not easily angered, it keeps no record of wrongs. Love does not delight in evil but rejoices with the truth. It always protects, always trusts, always hopes, always perseveres.

Love never fails. But where there are prophecies, they will cease; where there are tongues, they will be stilled; where there is knowledge, it will pass away. For we know in part and we prophesy in part, but when completeness comes, what is in part disappears. When I was a child, I talked like a child, I thought like a child, I reasoned like a child. When I became a man, I put the ways of childhood behind me. For now we see only a reflection as in a mirror; then we shall see face to face. Now I know in part; then I shall know fully, even as I am fully known.

And now these three remain: faith, hope and love. But the greatest of these is love.

I have stood in the rice paddies of Vietnam under heavy artillery attack. I have responded to the call of the first bombing of the World Trade Center—and helped rescue an expectant mother to ensure a little girl was born and survived. I have overcome the double agonies of segregation and poverty. I have overcome a drinking problem. I have been at Ground Zero. I have been crippled by the burdens of post-traumatic stress disorder. But by marrying again, I have said to all of these things that love is the greatest thing of all. And my wife gave me the greatest compliment of all when she told me that I have a special heart—the heart of a hero.

I'm not sure about that, but I'm glad that I found someone who thinks that much of me…because I feel the same about her.

About the Author

Clarence Singleton is a motivational speaker, author, a former United States Marine, a veteran of the Vietnam War, and a Purple Heart Medal recipient. Singleton is also a decorated former New York City Firefighter whose unit responded to the first attack on the World Trade Center in 1993, where he was credited with saving numerous lives. After retiring from the FDNY in 2000, Singleton volunteered for duty on September 11, 2001 at the World Trade Center, where he was seriously injured and was featured in *One Nation: America Remembers September 11, 2001* by the authors of *Life Magazine*.

One of eight children, Clarence Singleton was born in Sumter, South Carolina in 1949. After his father deserted the family when Singleton was six years old, he held numerous jobs (frequently being taken out of school) to help support his family while managing to keep his grades well above average. Before graduating from Lincoln High School in 1967, Singleton enlisted in the United States Marine Corps and was sent for recruit training at Marine Corps Recruit Depot Parris Island, South Carolina. During training, he was selected as the *Outstanding Member* of his platoon—an honor bestowed upon the recruit who most nearly attains the characteristics of an ideal United States Marine—and he was meritoriously promoted.

Singleton served in Vietnam as a Lance Corporal with the 2nd Battalion, 9th Marines. With only 28 days left in his tour of duty, Singleton received multiple wounds while trying to save lives during a 122mm rocket attack on his unit, which earned him the Purple Heart Medal. After more than a year of hospital care in Japan and the Charleston Naval Hospital, Singleton decided to redirect his life and moved to New York City where one of his older sisters lived.

In 1969 Singleton was employed by Manufacturers Hanover Trust Company where during his nine year tenure, worked his way up to supervisor of the Quality Control Section. Deciding to pursue a degree, Singleton enrolled in New York City Community College in 1975 while holding down his full time position. In 1978, he decided to join the New York City Fire Department.

During his 22 year tenure with the New York City Fire Department (FDNY), he received a number of awards for bravery and outstanding initiative. In 1993, he and his fire unit responded to the first attack on the World Trade Center where he was credited with saving numerous lives including that of a pregnant worker who went into labor during the attack. In 1994, Singleton was promoted to Fire Lieutenant and sent to supervise a firehouse in Bushwick, a sprawling neighborhood in the New York City borough of Brooklyn. In August, 2000, he retired from the FDNY.

When the World Trade Center was again attacked on September 11, 2001, donning his firefighter uniform Singleton voluntarily went to "Ground Zero" to help. Working at the base of the collapsed South Tower, along with another firefighter and a police officer, he extinguished numerous vehicle fires. While there, the second tower collapsed, seriously injuring Singleton. After being treated at a nearby hospital, Singleton made his way back to Ground Zero, seeing what he could do to help. Suffering from extensive injuries and post-traumatic stress disorder, Singleton decided to leave New York City and ultimately ended up in Midlothian, Virginia.

Singleton has delivered numerous inspirational speeches throughout the Mid-Atlantic. He has been featured in a number of regional publications and he has appeared on the *Montel Williams Show*, as well as several radio stations. For the past three years, Singleton has delivered the keynote address at the Chester County's Honor and Remembrance Ceremony, commemorating the anniversary of 9/11—the day that changed the world.

On September 11, 2012, starting a new chapter in his life, Singleton married Ms. Mary Jean Heyres.

War: Vietnam
  Awards and Commendations
    Purple Heart Medal
    National Defense Medal
    Republic of Vietnam Service Medal
    Vietnam Campaign Medal
    Conspicuous Service Medal (New York State)
    Certificate of Recognition for promoting peace and stability
      in the Nation
    Certificate of Appreciation, United States Senate
    Certificate of Appreciation, Disabled American Veterans
      Association

Awards and Commendations, New York Fire Department
    World Trade Center Rescuer Medal, Fire Department, the
      City of New York
    Unit Citation
    Class B Medal for Bravery
    Class B Medals for Initiative (two)
    World Trade Center Victim Flag by the House of
      Representatives

CPSIA information can be obtained
at www.ICGtesting.com
Printed in the USA
FFOW04n1819280216
21828FF